KT-509-069

LOST PERTH

*

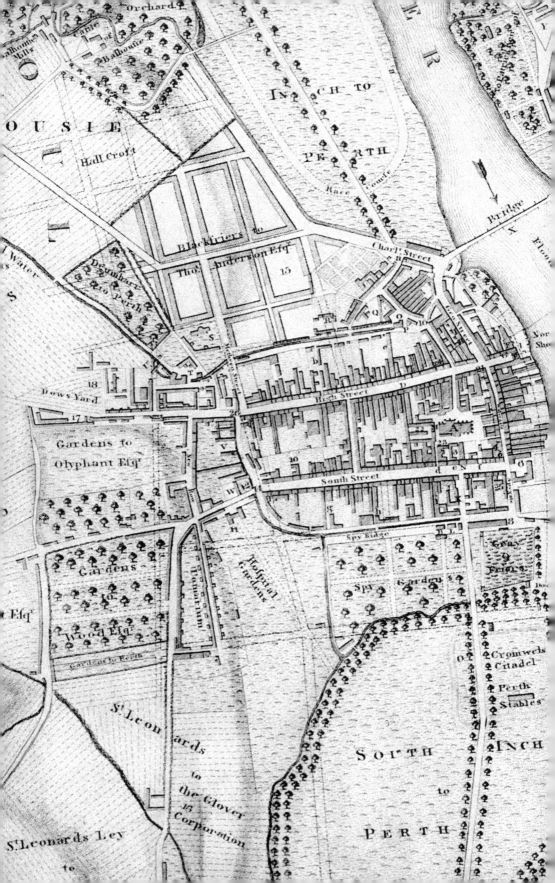

LOST PERTH

Jeremy Duncan

BIRLINN

PREVIOUS PAGE.

An extract from William Macfarlane's Plan of the Ancient Town of Perth, *1792.*
Courtesy of the AK Bell Library, Local Studies Department, Perth and Kinross Council

First published in 2011 by
Birlinn Limited
West Newington House
10 Newington Road
Edinburgh
EH9 1QS

www.birlinn.co.uk

Copyright © Jeremy Duncan 2011

The moral right of Jeremy Duncan to be
identified as the author of this work has been
asserted by him in accordance with the
Copyright, Designs and Patents Act 1988

All rights reserved. No part of this publication
may be reproduced, stored, or transmitted in
any form, or by any means, electronic,
mechanical or photocopying, recording or
otherwise, without the express written
permission of the publisher.

ISBN: 978 1 84158 966 4

British Library Cataloguing-in-Publication Data
A catalogue record for this book is available
from the British Library.

Design: Mark Blackadder

Printed and bound by Gutenberg Press, Malta

For Genevieve and Iain

CONTENTS

INTRODUCTION AND ACKNOWLEDGEMENTS

By exploring lost Perth – and so much of Perth has been lost – we can begin to understand what was important to the townspeople of old, how they thought, what they did and how they reacted to trends, events and change. For a town's buildings and, indeed, its customs and institutions, too, are ultimately a manifestation of an evolving municipal mindset and, by looking afresh at those now gone and the purposes they served, we can discover the deeper workings of the city and people of old Perth.

This book does not purport to be a record of every building that has disappeared from the streets of the city or every vanished pastime or organisation but it does aim at a broad-brush depiction of what were once regarded as the main buildings, places and institutions of the city. The principal sources used have been the minutes of the old Town Council of Perth, the newspapers of the city and the standard histories, details of which are provided in a separate bibliography. For the avoidance of excessive repetition, all unattributed quotes in the text are taken from the Town Council minutes.

All images are courtesy of Perth Museum and Art Gallery, Perth and Kinross Council except where stated. The *Perthshire Advertiser* owns the copyright in two of them and I express my thanks to the staff of this old Perth newspaper for permission to use them. Care has been taken not to infringe copyright, written or photographic, but, if I have done so unintentionally, then I apologise to anyone concerned.

A number of people have helped in the writing of this book and it is my pleasure to acknowledge them in print and thank them for their assistance. Of immense help during the several months of research were the staff of the AK Bell Library in Perth, principally those in the archive and local studies sections. It has been said, with justification, that the Perth archives are amongst the finest outside the capital and this is due to archivist Steve

Connelly, who so willingly imparts his extensive knowledge of both the city and the collection in his care, and to his very capable and welcoming assistants, Jan Merchant and Christine Wood. At the other end of the building, Sara Ann Kelly, local studies librarian, and her team of Yvonne Bell, Marjorie Donald and Anne Carroll have made their resources freely available to me and never once seemed flustered by yet another request for some obscure item from the stack. Across town, the photographic officer at Perth Museum and Art Gallery, Paul Adair, has been his usual kind and helpful self, gently nudging me in the right direction when the huge number of photographs he curates was threatening to become overwhelming. His colleagues in the reception area and elsewhere in the building were unfailingly cheery and I thank them all.

Several others have kindly assisted by providing particular pieces of information or offering photographs. They are the above-mentioned Steve Connelly, Stan Keay, Graham Mackenzie (hospital master of the King James VI Hospital), my neighbour Bill Robertson, Tommy Smyth (archivist of the Black Watch Museum), ex-Lord Dean of Guild Michael Thomson and John Wright of Glenalmond College. My grateful thanks go to them.

I am much indebted to both Ann Lindsay, author of the companion volume, *Lost Perthshire*, for her help, advice and encouragement, particularly in the early stages, and Tommy Smyth who read the chapter on Perth and the military and saved this distinctly non-military-minded author from some embarrassing mistakes. My mentor (if I may call her that), the indefatigable Rhoda Fothergill, has read almost the entire manuscript, corrected a number of errors and made many useful recommendations. I continue to be almost breathless with astonishment at the depth of her knowledge of Perth and am grateful for her willingness to share it. My warmest thanks to her. I should add, of course, that the responsibility for any remaining errors lies entirely with me.

And, finally, my family. My dear wife, Wendy, despite the pressures of a particularly demanding job, has been immensely supportive through the long months of research and writing, not only bringing coffee and sticky buns at opportune moments and assisting with the proof-reading but encouraging and cajoling whenever required. Words cannot adequately express how much I owe to her. Genny has been simply the best daughter any father could wish for and has made her old man very proud. I dedicate this volume to her and to Iain, my son-in-law, with much love.

CHAPTER 1

THE WATERWAYS OF PERTH

The great Victorian painter, Sir John Everett Millais, whose wife was a Perth girl, stood on Perth Bridge on a bright winter's morning and, gazing northwards towards the Highlands, memorably described the prospect as 'much better than the Riviera'. Little has changed today apart from the noise of the traffic on the bridge itself. Cross the road, though, and the view downstream would be virtually unrecognisable to Millais. Where now there exists the beautiful curve of Tay Street with its architecturally eclectic range of fine buildings, there was then a bowling green, a ramshackle collection of mainly industrial sheds, the twelve-seater public lavatories of the Diddledan, beached boats and open spaces sloping gently down to the river. Further on, if Millais had enjoyed good eyesight, he might have made out a number of half-finished wooden vessels in the shipbuilding yards. And where the river is now used by a few anglers and the occasional motorboat and jet ski, it had, within the recent memory of Millais's contemporaries, been busy with all sorts of craft, from tall-masted ocean-going vessels to small fishing cobles, making passage to or from the earlier harbours of Perth. The shore would have buzzed with the activity of loading and unloading, of carters hauling cargoes into the city itself and of seamen spending their hard-earned pay at the Shore Tavern.

Trade is the lifeblood of every economy and the Tay was one of the great arteries which facilitated the constant flow of goods into and out of Perth. Until the development of modern roads and railways, in the eighteenth and nineteenth centuries, boat was by far the quickest mode of transport and, bearing in mind the limitations of horse and cart, the best suited for bulk loads. A good example is provided by the trade in lime, a powdery substance which had a variety of important uses, not least of them as an agricultural fertiliser, as a mortar for building and, of course, as lime wash. Though some of the lime used in Perth came from the north of England, much of it was supplied from the Earl of Elgin's estates at Charleston in the south of Fife, a short distance of around 30 miles by car today. Yet, up to the nineteenth century – and possibly beyond – lime was delivered by boat, a voyage of upward of 80 miles which entailed sailing down the Forth, round the Fife headland and up the Tay, negotiating sandbanks and other river hazards on the way.

The earliest harbour, known latterly as the North Shore, was situated at the foot of the High Street, close to the heart of the town. Although not specifically mentioned in the charter of c. 1210 which confirmed Perth's royal burgh status, the presence of an early harbour is implied by several references to trading with foreigners as well as by recent archaeological evidence. The silting of the river, resulting from deforestation and agricultural improvements in the Tay catchment area, was a perennial problem for the town authorities

This rare view of Perth in the 1860s, before Tay Street was formed, is close to what Millais might have seen when crossing the bridge into Perth.

and was only resolved, in the short term, by building a new harbour further downstream. Although the North Shore remained in use by smaller vessels until the nineteenth century, the construction of the Council House across the foot of the High Street in the 1690s was proof indeed of its diminishing importance.

The South Shore or New Shore was established in the sixteenth century at the end of what is now Canal Street. At that time, though, as the street name implies, this was where a branch of the town lade debouched into the Tay. A military map of 1715–16 shows 'The Kay' as a sizeable basin, extending west from the river as far as Speygate. Despite the South Shore being enlarged in 1727, there was an ever-pressing need for further dock space and, by the end of the eighteenth century, the Coal Shore had been established a little

A late eighteenth century view of the North Shore, Perth's earliest harbour. The Council House can be seen on the right and the masts of a ship on the left. Courtesy of the AK Bell Library, Local Studies Department, Perth and Kinross Council

downstream of the South Shore, the Merchants Quay was flourishing by the South Inch and the Lime Shore occupied a stretch of the river bank even further south. These harbours served a booming trade not only with ports of the Forth and elsewhere around Britain but with those further afield, from Germany, Russia and Scandinavia to France, Spain and Italy.

The requirements of the city's importers for storage space at the harbours led to the construction of wood yards, warehouses, coal slips and lime sheds. Much trade was done at the harbours, often as soon as shipments arrived. Once deals were struck, goods had to be transported from the shore into town by carters and porters who were an integral part of life by the river. Reading between the lines of the carters' regulations and their frequent revisions, they were an argumentative bunch, lazy and prone to overcharging. The regulations of 1789, for example, required them to register with the Council, to take jobs in

A vessel lies moored at the Lime Shore, its cargo on the quay. Left of centre are telegraph poles and in the distance the spire of today's St Matthew's Church.

the order in which they were given and to take their stand at the Coal Shore in turn. Overloading of carts was prohibited. Fees were 5d per ton from the Coal Shore to anywhere in the town, with a little extra being charged for a journey beyond Meal Vennel. Porters, who provided a similar service but without carts, were a similar breed, licensed by the Council and identifiable by a badge with their particular number engraved on it. They were required to produce a character reference if asked, testifying to their honesty and good behaviour, and were forbidden from evading particularly onerous tasks by saying they were busy when they were not. Pay could range from a penny for placing a load of coal in a cellar to ten shillings for a full ten-hour day.

The busyness at the shore was supervised by Council officials such as the shore master and the berthing master, the latter in charge of providing moorings for shipping. In 1799, the Council appointed a second bulking master to hasten the loading and unloading of goods at the shore. Others, such as the tacksmen, who collected shore dues on behalf of the Council, and members of the Seamen's Society, who were authorised to collect one penny for every registered ton of shipping (the proceeds going towards keeping the river clear of obstructions), were perhaps less popular members of the shore community. With shipbuilders and masons engaged on regular harbour repairs and extensions, the shore, unlike today, was a busy part of town.

The main reasons why these once-busy old harbours have long since been abandoned were the losing battle against the silting of the river and the problems ever-larger vessels were having in navigating the river shallows. The Council knew only too well the vital importance to the local economy of keeping the river navigable and went to extraordinary lengths to ensure that shipping could sail as far as the landing stages and warehouses of Perth. In 1728, for example, they had a 'water plough' specially made in London and, in 1750, following real fears that the main channel of the Tay was about to be permanently blocked by silt, they attempted to divert water from the Willowgate (today this is the narrower channel between the east side of Moncreiffe Island and Kinnoull parish, though at that time it was taking a substantial part of the flow) into the main channel of the river, thus increasing its depth. On another occasion, when a ship ran aground on one of the fords at the South Shore, they ordered a new dredging machine to be made.

More drastic action was taken from the start of the nineteenth century. In co-operation with neighbouring landowners, some river islands, such as Sleepless and Balhepburn, were physically linked to the shore by building up the channel between the nearest bank and the island. Water which once flowed on both sides was thus forced into the main channel, whose depth was thereby increased. In 1801, 'several respectable gentlemen', aware that the levels of shipping in Perth were declining, petitioned the Council to build an artificial channel from the deep water of the Tay at Friarton to the harbours upstream, thus bypassing the considerable hazards of the shallow fords. The Council commissioned the Scottish civil engineer, John Rennie, then working in London, to survey the river and surrounding area and submit a feasibility report. It was even suggested that this artificial channel could link with the proposed Perthshire Canal which was intended to provide a navigable passage between Perth and Loch Earn. Neither Rennie's proposal nor the Perthshire Canal proceeded beyond the paper stage, though Rennie's was still being considered almost 20 years later.

A report of 1819 by George Alexander, inspector of the town's works, shows just how bad the situation was becoming. Surveying the river between

Perth and Newburgh, he pointed out that, at low water, the shallow known as the Town's Ford (roughly opposite County Buildings) was actually dry in places and that the average depth was a mere 18 inches. Stone cairns in the river, built by fishermen, were further hazards as were large stones beneath the surface, some of them deliberately dumped by shipping getting rid of ballast – perhaps to give their vessels greater clearance in such difficult waters.

In 1822, further pressure came in the form of a petition to the Council from 'a great number of the most respectable burgesses and traders within the city' stating their concern about the significant decline in shipping at Perth and the concomitant effect on local commerce. They too emphasised the problem of the shallows upstream of Newburgh and, while acknowledging the great expense of clearing the river and the poor state of civic finances, nevertheless begged the Council to spend a little money on deepening the channel near the Cow Inch (just south of the Lime Shore) and dredging the Weel Ford near Friarton. This, they said, would allow shipping to reach Perth at the lowest of neap tides and improve communication with Dundee by steamboat, which had by then become 'the most fashionable and economic mode of travelling'. The Council acceded to their request and applied to Dundee for the use of their dredging machine. Later that year, they acquired a water depth gauge which was placed in the Town's Ford, thus giving warning to shipmasters attempting to cross when the water level was too low. By 1825, they were threatening dire punishments for shipmasters caught dumping ballast, gravel and even ash from steamboats into the river. More significantly, though, they were giving serious consideration that year to abandoning the old harbours altogether and running a railway line (presumably with horse-drawn wagons) from the mouth of the River Earn to Perth, thus allowing shipping to offload well before the shallows of the Fair City.

Towards the end of 1826, the Council's navigation committee was considering four options: John Rennie's proposal to construct a canal from Friarton; another proposal to dredge the river and deepen the fords; a proposal for a wet dock at the confluence of the Tay and Earn, with a railway or canal link to Perth; and a plan to build a new harbour close to where the present harbour is today. Mainly for financial reasons, the Council opted for the second the dredging of the river and the deepening of the two most obstructive fords, the Weel Ford and the Town's Ford – as well as the extension of both the South Shore and the Coal Shore. It was agreed to petition parliament for a bill for this purpose and, in 1830, the lord provost and town clerk having travelled to London to give added weight to the petition, it successfully passed through parliament, and the Council were given the authority to proceed with the desired improvements.

In 1834, a further Harbour Act was passed, amending that of 1830, which gave the Harbour Commissioners (in whom, from 1830, the responsibility for the harbour had been vested) the authority to construct a tide harbour at Friarton and this developed into the modern harbour of today. While larger vessels were thereafter confined to Friarton, smaller boats continued to make use of the old harbours and indeed Lime Shore was still known as such until well into the twentieth century. In 1886, there was a successful application to the Town Council by the Dundee, Perth and Newburgh Steamboat Company to land and take on passengers at the foot of the High Street though it is difficult to imagine that this would actually have happened.

The town's river problems did not cease with the opening of the present harbour. Regular dredging of the channel downstream was still required and there were other obstacles too – not from natural hazards but from owners of riparian estates. In their ancient capacity as guardians of the river, the Council kept a close eye on works affecting it and, as it had done for centuries, stepped in very quickly when any potential threat to navigation was suspected. When Hay of Seggieden, for example, started building an embankment on the river or when Lord Dundas started erecting bulwarks in the Tay downstream of Newburgh and later when Richardson of Pitfour started works at Mugdrum Island, Council deputations were immediately despatched to inspect them. Some landowners would argue with the Council – as did Lord Kinnaird who strongly objected to the magistrates using a centuries-old privilege to take action against his harbour at Polgavie, though he was perhaps forgetting that his own station in life was similarly based on centuries-old privilege. The magistrates, however, stood firm. Prosecution was the ultimate course of action and the Council was never shy of taking this step. The issue was not simply one of threatened trade but a violation of ancient rights and privileges which had been conferred on the magistrates of Perth in medieval times by the kings of Scotland. The phrase 'conservators of the Tay' was regularly trotted out to remind trespassers of the town's ancient rights over the river, rights which extended as far as the old sheriffdom of Perth and therefore almost as far as Dundee itself. It is interesting to note that charters conferred in medieval times could effectively quash a proposed railway bridge over the Tay at Mugdrum in the 1840s and materially influence the design of the present Tay Bridge which was rebuilt in the 1880s, following the collapse of the original in 1879. The magistrates insisted that the central spans of this bridge be a certain height above high water, to allow shipping to proceed upstream to Perth, and even sent the burgh surveyor out in a boat to check the height for himself. He reported that the span was indeed a clear three inches above the minimum specified. The Council also tried to have the remaining stumps of the old bridge removed – those outwith the main navigable channel – but this was, almost literally, a bridge too far. The Board of Trade ultimately sided with the North British Railway Company, who owned the bridge, and stated that the stumps should stay as an additional warning to river traffic. Although beyond the bounds of the sheriffdom of Perth and thus the reach of Perth magistrates, Dundee Town Council was also closely watched. Whenever a bill went before parliament for improving the harbour at Dundee, the Perth Town Council's agents in London, Messrs Spottiswoode and Robertson, were instructed to keep a close eye on the progress of any legislation and ensure that none of Perth's rights was affected.

In the same way that larger shipping disappeared from the heart of Perth when the new harbour at Friarton opened, so the local ferry service disappeared as soon as the river was spanned by the new bridge of 1771. The rights to a ferry had long been held by the Town Council and, even though these boats had been in regular use on the Tay at Perth since the collapse of the last bridge in 1621, it seems to have occurred to the Council only as late as 1762 that money could be made from them. They had previously been licensed free of charge and without time limit but in that year, having spent money on addressing safety concerns and rebuilding the landing places, the Council resolved to levy a fee of ten shillings per year per boat. Detailed regulations were drawn up at the same time. Large boats, identified by a large painted L, had to be a minimum of 18 feet long and 9 feet wide, and wide at one end and narrow at the other. Small boats, prominently displaying a large S, could take, besides individual passengers, a maximum of two horses but never any cattle, carts or carriages. The ferry was required to operate primarily between the Gibraltar Quay (this little harbour was situated roughly opposite St Matthew's Church today and has since been incorporated into what is now the Norie Miller Riverside Walk) and the North Shore, though these locations could be varied in time of spate. The specified hours of operation were from 5 a.m. to 10 p.m. in the warmer months, with a shorter day permitted in winter. The late evening ferry service had to consist of four boats, two on each side of the river; whenever one boat set off with passengers, another on the opposite bank had to set off too, even if empty, in order to maintain an equal number of boats on each bank and thus minimise delays. The rates of crossing were also set out – each person to pay one farthing, each horse, ox or cow to cost one penny, each laden two-wheeled cart fourpence and each coach or chariot one shilling. When the river was in spate, the fare for individuals increased to one halfpenny and all other charges were increased by 50 per cent. In 1767, the

Council decided to auction the right to operate the ferries and one Thomas Stobb, a merchant, offered the sum of £50 5s sterling for the year ahead. This was accepted on condition that he operated a minimum of 12 large boats and 5 small and that they be kept in good repair.

An alternative ferry service was provided by the Stewart family, lairds of the Kincarrochy (now Kincarrathie) estate, whose boatmen plied between Tayfletts on the east bank of the river and the North Inch on the west. Kincarrochy paid nothing to the Council for the privilege of disembarking his passengers on town land and they eventually objected to this encroachment and threatened legal action against him. The dispute was settled in the town's favour by the arbitration of the eminent jurist, Duncan Forbes of Culloden, who ruled that Kincarrochy should pay the Council £2 per year to continue operating his ferry. Nothing, though, by way of collecting their dues seems to have been done until 30 years later when the Council realised that not a single

A scene of quiet industry at the harbour at Friarton, where railway goods wagons stand beside a ship, ready for loading.

Members of Perth Town Council in 1952, setting off in the Fair Maid *on their annual inspection of the river, exercising their ancient rights as conservators of the Tay. Note the crate of beer and international flags! Courtesy of the* Perthshire Advertiser *and Perth and Kinross Council Archive*

penny had been paid and they were now owed £60. When Kincarrochy objected to the demand for arrears, the case again went to law, which again went in the town's favour and the impecunious laird had to beg for time to pay. (The Kincarrochy affair was no isolated case; there were several other instances of poor financial management by the Council in the eighteenth century, one of which resulted in them having to pay a huge sum in back payments to the King James VI Hospital.)

The opening of the present Perth Bridge sounded the death knell for ferries at Perth; indeed several other ferries operating between Dundee and

Fife almost went out of business too, such was its impact on the area. In January 1771, the Bridge Commissioners resolved that, as the bridge was now passable for horses and carriages, all ferries within one mile upstream or downstream should cease after 26 January of that year. This, though, was already too late for the laird of Kincarrochy – as part of the bridge-building process a temporary wooden service bridge had already been constructed to which foot passengers were allowed access from Whitsunday 1768 at a rate of one farthing per single crossing. The traveller and writer Thomas Pennant described using this temporary bridge when he visited Perth at that time. In July 1768, Kincarrochy wrote to the Bridge Commissioners saying that his ferry was now 'quite laid aside and as effectually stopped as if the stone bridge were already finished and the same prohibited to be worked'. He had received no income at all since the service bridge had opened and was losing ten shillings per week. The matter was resolved reasonably amicably and he accepted the offer of £26 per year for 20 years as compensation.

Perth Bridge had several incarnations before the present one opened to travellers in January 1771. The earliest known, described by John of Fordun as 'the large bridge of St John', was swept away in 1209 by Perth's first recorded flood. All subsequent bridges, apart from the one still standing, appear to have followed the same line which crossed the river from a little to the north of the foot of the High Street, just upstream from the North Shore, in a north-easterly direction to the opposite bank.

This crossing of the Tay was of vital importance to the administration of the kingdom and Scottish kings made every effort, including contributions of large sums of money, to keep the bridge in good repair or, when disaster happened, to rebuild it. Robert the Bruce, for example, in 1328, the year before his death, ordered that stone be taken from the quarries of 'Kynkarachi et Balcormoc' for building the bridge at Perth. A charter of Robert III required that any fines imposed on those transgressing the charter of William the Lion of c. 1210 (which confirmed the privileges of a royal burgh) were to be put towards the upkeep of the bridge. And James VI, in Perth's Golden Charter of 1600, described it as 'a most precious jewel of our kingdom' and of prime importance in linking the two halves of the country, the Highlands and Lowlands.

The problem of maintaining a crossing at Perth is well illustrated by a difficult 50-year period in the late 1500s and early 1600s. In December 1573, a flood caused the collapse of two of the bridge's arches and, in January 1583, another flood swept away the bridge in its entirety. This seems to have been replaced initially by a wooden bridge, part of which collapsed in January 1599. There was another partial collapse two years later and, in February 1608, a build-up of ice took it away altogether. Work then began on a stone bridge. The keystone of the last arch was laid in 1616 and, in May of the following year, there is a reference to a stone representation of the king's arms being placed in position at the west end of the bridge near the tolbooth (one wonders, incidentally, if this stone carving gave its name to the nearby inn, the King's Arms). Despite the skill of John Mylne, master mason to the Crown of Scotland, the new stone bridge, low-built, could not withstand the volume of water pouring down the river following days of heavy rain and all but one of the eleven arches were swept away in October 1621. Shortly after this disaster, James VI, together with his son, the future Charles I, and several others contributed large sums towards its reconstruction but, even so, the funding was insufficient and the people of Perth, surely already disheartened by a seemingly losing battle against the river, remained without a bridge for almost 150 years.

It was perhaps ironic that the first railway bridge at Perth, a flimsy wooden structure, was opened at the height of the January 1849 flood. The local dignitaries at the opening, whose role it was to traverse the bridge, could not have been unaware of what had happened to earlier wooden bridges in time of flood. With the main channel of the Tay thundering beneath them and the whole area between the station at Barnhill and the General Station on the far side of the South Inch beneath water, they must have ventured across with some trepidation.

The story of this bridge began in the mid 1840s when four railway lines, built by four different railway companies, were about to converge on Perth. Permission had initially been granted by the Council for a joint station on the South Inch, a hugely controversial decision that was ultimately withdrawn, though the price of withdrawal was high. In return for the Dundee and Perth Railway accepting this change of heart, the Council were obliged to support their proposal for a railway bridge across the Tay at Perth, a station at Princes Street and a viaduct continuing the line, behind Marshall Place, to the new (and present) site of the General Station at the west of the South Inch. This was a high price indeed as the Council had already objected to the same railway company's plan to cross the Tay further downstream at Mugdrum on the grounds that such a bridge would infringe their rights over the Tay, an objection which was upheld by the authorities in London. With the bargaining done, work began on the bridge in 1848.

Consisting of 25 arches built on timber piles and with a height of around 16 feet above the high water mark, the new bridge failed to inspire confidence from the start. Trains were restricted to a speed of eight miles per hour and, six months after opening, the Board of Trade, following an inspection, recom-

The first railway bridge at Perth was a short-lived wooden construction. It looks solidly built from this foreshortened viewpoint, but there were concerns about its strength from earliest days.

mended that the structure be strengthened to avoid the risk of collapse. An incident the following year would have done little to improve matters – a train collision at Barnhill resulted in a runaway and driverless engine careering at considerable speed over the bridge, straight through the new Princes Street station, and heading along the new viaduct towards the General Station where a train from Edinburgh was disgorging its passengers. A quick-witted pointsman managed to divert the train into a siding at the last moment, thus averting disaster. By 1859, the bridge was in such poor condition that the speed limit was further reduced to four miles per hour. The constant flexing of the timbers caused by the weight of trains resulted in significant wear and tear not only to the wooden structure but to the rails as well and, in a further attempt to minimise damage, the second track was removed. By 1862, the decision had been made to replace it with a stone bridge which was duly built by a London firm for around £24,000 and opened in late 1863. It remained a single-track bridge and, as with the old bridge, had a moveable arch to allow shipping to proceed upstream.

Chronologically, the next bridge over the Tay at Perth was first proposed

The Victoria Bridge in winter. This inelegant structure was replaced by the more fluid lines of the present Queen's Bridge in 1960.

in 1887. There had long been a need for a river crossing for the southern part of town and, indeed, in 1829, one of the Perth newspapers voiced the suggestion that a resumption of ferry services from County Buildings might be appreciated by visitors to Kinnoull. Ferry or no ferry, this was the site chosen for what became the Victoria Bridge, work on which began following the successful passage through parliament of the City Improvement Bill in 1897. Parliament, however, was not so much of an obstacle as a certain John Rollo whose home, Rodney Lodge, was scheduled to be demolished to make way for the new crossing. He was joined in opposing it by several others on the Kinnoull side of the river who felt that the amenity of their expensive villas would be threatened by this unexpected proximity to the South Street area, one of the poorer parts of Perth. Rollo put up a strong fight but it was a lost war and, in 1898, with work on the bridge's foundations and the approach road from Dundee already underway, he accepted compensation of just under £4,000, less than 20 per cent of what he had originally claimed. With the loss of such a splendid dwelling, in a prime riverside location and the minimal compensation offered, one can understand his subsequent action in refusing to

One of the remaining gable ends of Rodney Lodge which flanked the Victoria Bridge until the 1930s.

make available an inch more than was absolutely necessary for the new bridge. The result was that the gable ends of Rodney Lodge remained standing for the next 30 or so years. It perhaps did not matter too much as the bridge itself was no object of beauty and, when, in 1960, the substantial stone piers and high metal sides of the Victoria Bridge were replaced by the rather more graceful profile of the Queen's Bridge, it was not greatly mourned.

The 1940s witnessed a short-lived bridge over the Tay between the North Inch and the grounds of what is now Upper Springland. This wooden structure, built by the military during the war, appears on an Ordnance Survey map of 1949 and was presumably demolished shortly after.

There were many more bridges in Perth, not over the Tay but spanning the other waterway of the city, the town's lade. Many today will know the lade as that gently flowing stream behind the Dunkeld Road but, prior to the twentieth century, this watercourse was one of the main engines of the city's economy, providing direct water power to the mills and many local businesses and manufacturing industries and later, from around the 1830s, supplying water to drive the ever-increasing number of steam engines that were becoming part of the manufacturing process. The origins of the lade are unclear. It is assumed to be a man-made channel, dug in early medieval times, before the earliest records of the town were written, to provide power for the town's mills. Extending to around four miles in length and running from the River Almond to the Tay, it must have been a huge enterprise for the time. An alternative explanation would have to be that it was a natural channel, since straightened in places and greatly canalised, either an offshoot from the Almond or perhaps even at one time the original course of that river. From the Almond, the lade takes a winding course towards Perth before dividing at the Boot of Balhousie. The main channel flows through the town's mills and along the side of Mill Street, before joining the Tay just downstream of Perth Bridge from where its wide culvert is clearly visible. The Balhousie branch flowed along the west side of the North Inch before rejoining the main branch just before it entered the Tay.

From near the mills, another branch followed the line of Methven Street, Canal Crescent and Canal Street before entering the Tay at the end of today's Canal Street, where the South Shore had once been. This Canal Street branch also diverged with another offshoot flowing behind the houses of James Street (on its eastern side) towards Marshall Place and from there, after a little dog-leg to the west, round the western side of the South Inch to join first the Craigie Burn and then the Tay at Friarton. Central Perth was thus surrounded by water, which may explain why the lade was once described by a seven-teenth-century French mapmaker as a moat. It is indeed conjectured that the Canal Street branch was constructed as a defensive measure by the English army of occupation in the early fourteenth century.

To travel out of the city, to access the Inches or just to visit the houses and flats of Castlegable or the Old High Street or Newrow or Rose Terrace, one had to cross a bridge. Those distinguished with a name included the Union Bridge, which crossed the lade at the junction of Mill Street and Kinnoull Street, before the latter was extended to link up with Scott Street, the Turret Brig at the High Street Port, roughly where St Paul's Church now stands (and, if you look up at this building, you will see a small plaque on the wall indicating the proximity of the lade), and the Red Brig at the north end of Skinnergate which was once one of main approaches to Perth. Others were built by local businesses such as Pullars and Campbells, by the residents of Rose Terrace, by Perthshire Cricket Club and by the Royal Perth Golfing Society, to name but a few. This last-mentioned bridge, made in 1879 of decorative ironwork, was for the convenience of club members wishing to access the North Inch and was specially made in Glasgow at a cost of £50. Many more were probably little more than a couple of planks, costing a few pennies, allowing access to a home or place of work. One bridge, built at the Free West Church in Mill Street in 1843, actually extended along the whole frontage of the church and was in reality not so much a bridge as a partial covering of the lade. All such bridges had to be authorised by the Council who exacted a nominal annual rent and retained the right to have the bridge removed at any time. Other bridges were thrown across the lade without any permission being sought or granted and, every so often, the Council would check and remove unauthorised ones.

As with any watercourse, the lade was potentially dangerous. Despite regular complaints about the flow being barely sufficient to drive machinery, it was still powerful enough to carry away those unfortunate enough to fall in, whether they were children playing during the day or drunken adults making their way home at night. Added to the danger of drowning was the awful prospect of being swept under a waterwheel, an experience which not many survived. The lade, however, was also used by residents as a convenient source of water, latterly for washing rather than drinking, and, in several places, steps were provided to allow access to the water from the street. By the eighteenth century, the Council had started to wall in the lade in an attempt to reduce the number of fatalities and this was the beginning of the process which has led to its virtual disappearance from view. Such walls were not always popular and, in the 1830s, lengthy petitions of complaint were presented to the Council. Some residents even threatened legal action while others simply knocked them down at night in a reaffirmation of what they felt was their right of access to lade water. Some, on the other hand, were in favour of protective measures. According to the *Perthshire Courier*, one petition, from 'several influential gentlemen' to the Lord Advocate in 1874, drew his attention to 'the unprotected and dangerous state' of the lade in a densely populated part of the city. The walls were low and insecure and of little protection even to young children. Two mill wheels were entirely exposed to passers-by and the stream was described as broad, deep and rapid. Only days earlier, a small boy had fallen in, been swept under a mill wheel, then under a covered section, and eventually out into the Tay. It was, though, useful for would-be suicides, such as the female ballad singer who in 1837 threw herself in above the Union Bridge, only to be hauled out – alive, well and furious – a little below Pullars' dye works. Despite the protests, however, and the eventual covering over of the lade in central Perth, there were still long stretches of it visible in the suburbs and the tragic drownings were almost as frequent. In 1949, the Perth Trades and Industrial Council tried putting pressure on the Town Council – unsuccessfully – to fence the lade at Tulloch, pointing out that, in the previous

A print of the 1840s showing Georgian Perth in all its splendour. Old Perth, though, lurks to the left of the bridge where a smaller bridge over the lade can be seen. Courtesy of the AK Bell Library, Local Studies Department, Perth and Kinross Council

15 years, there had been 15 accidents of which six had proved fatal.

The first steps to cover over the lade, rather than merely wall it in, were also taken in the eighteenth century and were the beginning of a process which has left only small parts of it still visible in central Perth. The Canal Street branch of the lade was wider than that of Mill Street and went by the name of the South Stank. This sluggish stretch of water was not, and could not have been, used for water power and was therefore a prime candidate for being arched over. The first section to be covered, in 1791, was between Speygate and Princes Street, this being adjacent to the South Shore quay and therefore a busy harbour area. Three years later, another section, opposite the riding school and therefore roughly where Love's Auction Rooms used to be, was covered over and in 1801 the proprietors of what was now being called Canal Street petitioned the Council to permit the arching over of the rest of the South Stank. By 1807, it seems that virtually the entire length of the Canal Street branch of the lade, from Methven Street to the river, had disappeared, with the exception of access points to the water which the Council had insisted on.

Atholl Place, separated from the North Inch by Charlotte Street, the old railings and the Balhousie branch of the lade. The watercourse disappears underground where the stone pillar stands.

The lade in Mill Street was covered over in piecemeal fashion during the nineteenth century. The section in front of the Free West Church was covered in 1843, that between Methven Street and Kinnoull Street a year or two later (as part of the construction of the public baths and wash house) and the long stretch between Kinnoull Street and Curfew Row in the 1860s when Pullars acquired all the land north of the lade and built new premises over it.

The Marshall Place section was arched over during the course of building what was then the Free St Leonard's Church (now St Leonard's-in-the-Fields) in the 1880s, the only dissenting voice on the Council being that of Magnus Jackson, the eminent Perth photographer, whose house bordered the lade and whose studio was demolished to make way for the church. The section between Canal Street and Marshall Place was filled in shortly after, with the water being conveyed underground in large pipes. The South Inch section, between Marshall Place and the Craigie Burn, was presumably covered over at around the same time and certainly by the end of the century. That stretch of the Balhousie lade bordering the North Inch remained open until the middle

Council officials inspecting the lade near Tulloch.

of the twentieth century and is still remembered by some of the city's older residents. Judging by photographs, it had been an attractive adornment of the Inch.

The provision of a drinkable supply of water to the Perth population, the diminution in importance of waterpower to industry, safety concerns and sheer convenience have all contributed to the gradual covering over of the lade in central Perth. The removal of the harbour to Friarton and the recent building of the flood defence walls indicate a similar turning away from the river on which Perth, until the development of the railway, had been so dependent. The Tay will continue to flow but not so, perhaps, the lade. At the time of writing in early 2011, the lade at Low's Wark, the point where water is channelled from the River Almond, was reported to be bone dry, resulting from its dilapidated state. There was, however, water in the lade at Perth but it could only have come from the land drains of farms further upstream. The city fathers of old, who made such efforts to keep the lade open, most certainly would not have approved.

CHAPTER 2

THE LOST
INDUSTRIES OF PERTH

From both angling and culinary perspectives, the Tay is one of the world's great rivers for salmon. As any angler, fishmonger or restaurateur will tell you, salmon from the Tay sells at a premium. Though now regarded by some as a sport for the well-off, salmon fishing for much of Perth's history had been hard, cold and wet labour. Yet it was also a lucrative source of revenue for the town, which benefited from the lease of its fishing rights and from the wealth created by the enormous demand in London and overseas for the king of fish. For many years, it was Perth's prime export, thanks, in part, to the continual efforts made by the Council to maintain a navigable link with the outside world.

The Perth fishings, which mainly lay within the royal burgh boundary but also included some of the river islands downstream such as Insherrit and Sleepless, had become big business by the eighteenth and nineteenth centuries. The Council widely advertised the leases in the press and wealthy merchants, some from as far away as London, put in their best offers for them. In 1817, for example, the fishings were let to John Bell, a merchant in Berwick, for £1,485 per year for seven years, a figure which today would equate to approximately £90,000 per year.

The one man most closely associated with the fish trade in Perth was John Richardson, the son of a local baker who eventually made a fortune from it, built a home at Pitfour Castle and whose descendants, having married into the Stewart of Urrard family and taking the name Stewart-Richardson, acquired both a double-barrelled name and a useful baronetcy. Beginning his career as a tacksman of the town's fishings in 1757, he branched out into buying fish from other fishermen, eventually sourcing from all over Scotland and exporting to the huge market in London. There were, however, irritating consequences for the citizens of his hometown, as is described in 1806 in *Memorabilia of Perth*:

23

During the season of salmon-fishing, a walk on the North Inch has an additional interest. In good seasons, thirty, forty, or fifty salmon are sometimes taken at one haul; and there have been instances of a number much and incredibly larger. The vast quantity of this exquisite fish which the river annually produces, is mostly consumed in London; and the inhabitants of Perth justly complain of the difficulty they have in procuring a dish which nature has provided them. This arises from the circumstance of all the fishings in the neighbourhood being farmed by two houses only, who find it in their interest to forward a regular supply to the London market.

Exporting fish to London by ship – a journey that could take anything from two and a half days to a week – was a risky business and, for obvious reasons, was initially carried on in the colder months. In the second half of the eighteenth century, however, the development of new methods of preservation not only allowed the London trade to continue throughout the fishing season but also opened up new markets overseas. The salting of salmon, which kept them edible for longer, brought continental markets within John Richardson's reach, some as far afield as southern Europe. His ships, on their return journey, would regularly stock up with supplies of salt from Lisbon. In 1796, as much as 17,000 bushels of salt were offloaded at Perth, a significant proportion of which would presumably have gone for salting salmon. The pickling of salmon, by parboiling and then barrelling in vinegar, was also successful though the result was apparently more to the taste of Europeans than Londoners. The most effective method, however – one which was suggested to Richardson by George Dempster of Dunnichen in the 1780s – was preservation in ice. In this way, fish could be sold as fresh and thereby achieve a higher price. Such methods allowed the salmon industry to flourish, keeping between 200 and 300 fishermen in employment on the Tay and providing enough trade to keep six ships in constant communication with London.

By the turn of the nineteenth century, though, the Perth salmon industry was facing the first of a series of challenges. The traditional method for fishing had been by net and coble, by which one end of a net was attached to a small boat, or coble, and the other end held by a man on the shore. Together they would stretch out the net and, moving in tandem, sweep as much of their part of the river as possible. While this was effective where the river was relatively narrow, it was less so in the estuary, a problem which the stake net method attempted to solve. Stake nets were left in the river estuary semi-permanently and netted huge numbers of fish when the tide went out. They required less effort and enabled fishermen to cover a much wider area of the river. Naturally this had a particularly adverse effect on the numbers of salmon reaching the narrower waters near Perth. In the first few years after this method was introduced, the number of salmon caught in the river fishings – as opposed to those of the estuary – dropped by 80 per cent. John Richardson was one of the first to complain about this and urged other river proprietors, such as Lord Kinnoull, Lord Gray, Sir Thomas Moncreiffe and, of course, the town itself, to take legal action. Such recourse was ultimately successful and stake nets were removed from the river by 1817. They were, however, permitted in coastal waters and, in the middle of the century, the estuarial proprietors came back with a different type of net which was declared legal in spite of the protestations of proprietors further upstream.

Such developments led to a decline in salmon numbers in the nineteenth century and the Town Council looked favourably on any measure designed to reverse such a threat to the town's livelihood. They supported bills in parliament for improving salmon fisheries on the Tay, they contributed towards the costs of protecting salmon in the close season at the same time, perhaps conversely, as campaigning for a longer open season and they followed, with interest, the experiments in the artificial propagation of salmon at the fishponds at Stormontfield. But it was never quite enough and, on occasion, they had to allow rebates to the tacksmen of the fishings by way of compensation for the low numbers of salmon caught.

Many of the Tay fishings in the later nineteenth century, excluding those of the town, were amalgamated in the Tay Salmon Fisheries Company which took a more balanced and long-term view of river fishing. Even so, a century later and despite better river management, continued net fishing was resulting in continually dwindling salmon stocks. To combat this, the Tay Foundation was set up to buy out the nets on the lower sections of the river and, by the end of the twentieth century, had either purchased or leased the rights to all net fishings on the Tay, including the town fishings of Perth which they took over on a 99-year lease.

Several buildings in Perth were associated with the fishing industry, such as the fishing lodges which provided a degree of shelter for those at work on the river. The accommodation was basic, though, and frequently the subject of complaints from the tacksmen. Londoner Matthew Bell who acquired the tack

OVERLEAF. *A group of salmon fishermen on the shores of the Tay, just downstream of Perth, with their traditional equipment of nets and boats. This photograph was probably taken around 1870.*

in 1824 complained about the state of the lodges at Sleepless Island and the Council duly authorised replacements. Another was described in 1857 as being frequently flooded by the tide and therefore very damp and, at only 12 feet square, somewhat cramped. As there were also three beds for six men to share, the remaining space for a fire and for cooking was limited in the extreme. Its comforts were further enhanced by wind blowing through the walls and rain dripping through the roof. Another lodge at the top of the North Inch was likewise an object of no great beauty. Following complaints in 1847, the Council informed Sir John Richardson that it should be 'in keeping with the beauty of the locality in which it stands' and asked him either to remove or improve it. He opted for the latter.

The fish market was situated in the Watergate prior to its removal to the foot of the High Street in 1788 and then, following several complaints, to the North Shore in 1818. This old harbour is presumably where salmon were landed, the water being deep enough to provide sufficient draught for cobles. The market itself was where the present Council headquarters is situated and consisted of sheds with booths for fishmongers. When the site was acquired for a new Post Office in around 1861 it seems that the fish market moved to a new spot just south of County Buildings. It was unlikely ever to have lasted long in that situation, though, as the developing elegant promenade of Tay Street, where even telegraph wires were laid underground to obviate the need for poles, would not have been regarded by the city fathers as a suitable location for the carts, smells and language of a fish market. It was seemingly closed permanently around 1870.

Elsewhere along the riverside, particularly where Tay Street was to be built, there were sheds for boiling fish, for storing ice and for packing, all functions of the once-busy export process. Though contributing as they did to the wealth of Perth, they created a significant eyesore when viewed from the bridge, one of the principal approaches to the town. There was doubtless a great sigh of relief among the city fathers when what had been described in the press as 'a disgrace' was finally cleared away. Gone too are the cobles which trawled the Tay at Perth and the nets on the North Inch, which were once a common sight. All that remains is the occasional hardy angler standing up to his waist in the cold waters of the Tay at Perth.

It is quite possible that the flourishing export trade in fish may have spawned Perth's other river-based industry – shipbuilding. With busy harbours supporting a flourishing maritime trade, it was perhaps a wise move for the Council, in 1768, to have offered a financial incentive to encourage a ship's carpenter to move to Perth. Although the plan may initially have been to have

Believed to be the Ballinbreich Castle, *which was the last sailing ship to be built in Perth. It was launched in 1879. Courtesy of the AK Bell Library, Local Studies Department, Perth and Kinross Council*

someone to hand capable of carrying out repairs to local shipping, it seems to have led directly to the start of shipbuilding in the town. The offer was taken up by one David Gibson and, almost 40 years later, in 1807, he was still running a shipyard at the Lime Shore. According to George Penny, in *Traditions of Perth*, the incentive was paid for many years until Gibson requested permission to build a house on some ground he owned. The Council, taking the view that, if he had sufficient funds to build a house, then he had no further need of 'incentives', stopped the payments forthwith. Although its beginnings in the last quarter of the eighteenth century were slow the evidence suggests that by the early to mid nineteenth century, the industry was gathering momentum. Certainly the Council was in receipt of requests for additional space for shipbuilding and, perhaps in response, had fenced off part of the Cow Inch for this purpose. By 1841, there were six shipyards, by 1847 nine and by 1860, according to a detailed Ordnance Survey map, there was an extensive area of yards almost due east of Perth Prison. Shipbuilding was also carried out at Bridgend, a little upstream of the Queen's Bridge of today.

The growth of shipbuilding in Perth is reflected in the statistics. In the 20 years between 1799 and 1818, a total of 15 boats were launched from the riverbank. In the next 20-year period, 97 were built and, in only four years, from 1839 to 1843, a remarkable total of 57. If any single day could be said to mark the industry's apogee, then it would have to be 28 August 1840. Not only were three ships launched on this sunny afternoon, with huge crowds watching, but the largest ship to have been built in Perth was one of them. This was the 445-ton barque, *Mary Gray*, which almost immediately set sail for London before beginning work as a passenger and goods ship on the high seas. Two years after her launch, she was recorded as setting out across the Pacific from Sydney to Valparaiso. Although many Perth ships were destined to work locally, ferrying coal or lime for example, a few, like the *Mary Gray*, sailed the shipping lanes of the world. *Mary Gray*, incidentally, was named after a Perthshire woman and was but one of several locally built ships so named to reflect their origins. Others included *Bellwood* (1803), *Friends of Perth* (1817), *Tay* (1819), *Lord Lynedoch* (1828), *St Johnstone* (1831), *Fair Maid* (1833), *Fox Maule* (1835), *Perthshire* (1836), *City of Perth* (1838) and *Simon Glover* (1840).

In the mid 1840s, the number of ships built in Perth declined significantly. One probable reason was that world economies, including the British, were in recession. Another may have been the several railways in the Perth area that were at the planning stage, perhaps giving businessmen, who had previously sent goods by ship, reason to wonder if rail, when it came, might be significantly faster. (It is noteworthy that the Council, in some matters, adopted a wait-and-see policy at this time, unsure of the effect the railway would have on trade.) Productivity picked up again, though, and shipbuilding as a significant Perth industry survived until the 1870s, at which time such businesses are no longer listed in local directories and advertisements begin to appear in the press for sales of shipyard stock. Statistics of Scottish shipbuilding for 1867 show that Perth built 14 ships in that year, which certainly bears comparison with the figure for 30 years earlier, but they were sailing ships and made of wood, whereas the shipyards of Glasgow, Port Glasgow, Greenock and Dundee were churning out steam vessels made of iron in great numbers.

While the shipbuilding and fishing industries in Perth were dependent on the river, many more were reliant on the town's lade, this watercourse providing both motive power and a water supply for the concentration of mills and industrial premises along its banks. The main reason for digging the channel, assuming it is not a natural waterway, was to provide water power to the oldest of these concerns, the town mills, which have had a history almost

The old malt barn which stood on the corner of Mill Wynd and West Mill Street, pictured in the 1930s. It was one of several such buildings clustered around the City Mills.

as long as the town itself. Forming a cluster around the lade at the north-west of the old town were mills for grinding wheat, barley and oats and associated buildings such as kilns for drying barley and granaries for storage. What is now the Tourist Information Centre in the Lower City Mills previously consisted of two mills – a corn mill to the north and a barley and malt mill to the south – with the mill wheel in the middle supplying power to both. The stone building attached to it on the south-east corner was originally a kiln. A few yards upstream were the upper and lower flour mills, now combined into a hotel. They were described in 1847 as old and rather cramped for working, though with several extensive granaries nearby – some now converted into flats and offices – the employees were spared the need to store grain in the mill buildings themselves.

The mills were generally leased for lengthy terms to the highest bidder, and while they provided a good income for the town, they could also, at times, be problematical. The buildings and machinery were constantly in need of repair, there were regular complaints from the tacksmen about the poor flow of water, the bakers of Perth complained about the burden of thirlage to the mills and there were fires, not infrequently resulting from carelessly supervised kilns. The waterwheels finally stopped turning as late as 1953 and the mills closed in 1966, lying empty until restoration in the 1980s.

Downstream there were several other mills, serving a variety of purposes. They included a waulk mill for the town's dyers, a cotton-spinning mill, which was later converted to wool-spinning, and sawmills, one of which was erected in 1836 at the very foot of the lade, virtually adjacent to Perth Bridge. There were complaints about its appearance but the response seems to have been that it was no less attractive than the fishing lodges on the North Inch. There were also mills associated with the town's linen industry, such as those for spinning flax and extracting linseed oil. The flax mill tenant, Thomas Fleming, was the subject of numerous complaints about the mill being worked at night and was threatened with eviction on at least one occasion unless he restricted working hours to between 6.00 a.m. and 8.00 p.m. On a later occasion, when faced with a backlog of work, he asked the Council for permission to work through the night, offering to muffle the sound of machinery with cushions.

The biggest enterprise to make use of the Mill Street lade was Pullars, one of the major employers in Perth and one of the best known dyeing and dry-cleaning firms in the world. John Pullar set up a dyeing business in 1824 in Burt's Close which was parallel to, and a little to the west of, Guard Vennel. The firm later moved across the lade and, in the 1860s, having acquired all the land between Kinnoull Street and Curfew Row, built a new works incorporating the lade within its walls. In 1918, after a long and distinguished history which was sadly marred at the end by violent industrial action, the company was taken over in a gentlemanly fashion by Eastman and Sons of London, though the business name survived until the later twentieth century. The Kinnoull Street–Mill Street premises, now known as Pullar House, have since been converted into office space for several Perth and Kinross Council departments, though without that famous Perth landmark, the Pullars' chimney, which was dismantled in 1980. Pullars itself was responsible for the disappearance of a number of old Perth buildings. As the firm expanded its Mill Street operations eastwards, across Curfew Row, it demolished the Free West Church, the above-mentioned flax mill and several other buildings too, including a tannery which, in 1849, had been recorded as exporting several thousand pounds worth of boots and shoes to London. Pullars established a major presence at the north-western edge of the city, again adjacent to the lade, when it took over the long-established Tulloch bleachfields in 1882.

Immediately upstream from the town's mills and accessed from Paul

An aerial view showing the full extent of Pullars city-centre operations. The factory was bounded by Kinnoull Street, Mill Street, Castlegable, Cherry Lane and Union Street.

OVERLEAF. *An interior view of Campbell's Dye Works.*

Street was the Perth Foundry which dated from 1820, though the building, as a former waulk mill, was somewhat older. The more northerly part of the lade, upstream from the barracks, was harnessed in the later nineteenth century, particularly that stretch on the west side of the Dunkeld Road which had hitherto been open land. Laurence Pullar, son of the above-mentioned John, went into partnership with Andrew Coates to form a successful jute-spinning and carpet-weaving business which flourished at the Balhousie Works from the 1870s. Next to the Balhousie Works, proceeding northwards, were the Perth Dye Works of P. & P. Campbell which were taken over by John Pullar and Sons following a disastrous fire in 1919. To the north of Campbell's Dye Works were the Wallace Works, the sole survivor of Perth's once vibrant linen-weaving industry. The works, established in 1851 by Fifers John and Alexander Shields, were initially in Foundry Lane from where, after a brief sojourn in Kinnoull Street, they moved to a brand-new factory at the ladeside which was opened

in 1869. The disappearance of most of these factories from the west side of the Dunkeld Road and subsequent replacement by a retail park and modern business premises have opened up and significantly improved this northern approach to Perth.

Of the southern-most branch of the lade, the most controversial building to make use of its water was Robert Storer's farina mill on the South Inch, close to the Craigie Burn. It was erected in 1853 with a view, perhaps, to manufacturing starch for either the local linen industry or local laundries. Whatever its purpose, complaints were pouring into the Council after only two days of operation. The potato-crushing engine was apparently discharging foul-smelling waste water into drains which eventually fed into the open lade, thus affecting much of southern Perth with its offensive odour. Despite it developing into a long-running dispute in which legal proceedings were threatened on several occasions, Storer was sufficiently well regarded to be co-opted onto the Town Council in 1861. The South Inch lade also powered a bruising mill (for grain) and, at the southern end, a cotton carding mill, the removal of which, in 1803, was intended to reduce the risk of flooding on the Inch.

The original function of the Balhousie lade was to power the Balhousie flour and meal mills and it seems to have done little else apart from supplying water to a snuff mill which was erected at the North Port in 1734. This was later converted into a sawmill before being demolished to make way for the handsome late-Georgian building on the corner of North Port and Charlotte Street.

Several other mills underwent changes of use, including a sawmill at the Red Brig which became a wheat mill, a nearby waulk mill which became a sawmill and an oil mill which was converted into a mill for crushing bones, much to the annoyance of the residents of nearby Castlegable. Such adaptability enabled local businesses to make use of the lade until recent times and, indeed, a report of 1961 indicated that it was still being used for industrial purposes by seven large businesses, which were drawing 40,000 gallons from it per day.

Perth's sudden transformation in 1848 into a major hub on the developing railway system opened up bright new vistas for local business. Add to this the arrival of the telegraph a few years later and the communications revolution with the rest of the country was well underway. By the early 1870s, a letter posted in Aberdeen in the late afternoon would be delivered in London by the following morning – a significant improvement on the old mail coach which would have taken at least two days. And, of course, a telegram was even quicker.

Several major Perth businesses became national names, owing to their astute use of new technologies. Pullars was one, quickly establishing a network of branches and agencies throughout Britain, which brought in items for dyeing and dry-cleaning locally before sending them off to Perth by rail for processing. The firm's premises at Tulloch were connected by a siding to the railway network. Two of Perth's big whisky names, Bells and Dewars, developed from local shops into worldwide brands, thanks to enterprising selling and the use of the railway. Bells, with premises in Victoria Street, Charles Street and latterly at Cherrybank, positioned themselves towards the south of the town while Dewars opted for the north, with premises on the Glasgow Road and, more recently, at Inveralmond. One of Perth's most recognisable landmarks was the massive red-brick bonded warehouse, close to the railway, on the corner of Glasgow Road and Glover Street which was first mooted in 1892 though only completed in 1912. Tall and rectangular, with turreted corners and the Dewar name blazoned in white brick on all sides, it dominated the surroundings in the manner of a medieval castle. Dewars, like Bells, no longer has a presence in Perth, the immense warehouse having been demolished in 1988 and the Inveralmond works around ten years later.

Perth was almost as well known across the globe for its pedigree bull sales which were generally held twice a year by livestock auctioneers Macdonald Fraser. Founded in Mill Street in 1864, the firm moved to a large site at Caledonian Road, adjacent to the railway, some 11 years later. With animal pens next to railway sidings and plenty of space for expansion, the company was well placed to take advantage of the developing railway network to bring in large numbers of animals for auction from across Scotland and further afield. Taken over by United Auctions in 1962, the company was forced by the Beeching cuts of that period to re-evaluate its reliance on the railway network and subsequently switched to road transport instead. No longer tied to the railway, the company moved, in 1989, from the Perth Auction Mart at Caledonian Road to the Perth Agricultural Centre at East Huntingtower. The link with Perth was virtually severed in 2009 when United Auctions left the city and based themselves in Stirling. Such was their fame, though, that the sales of bulls which now take place in that city are still known as the Perth Bull Sales. Today the Caledonian Road site is occupied by a branch of the supermarket chain, Morrisons, while Sainsbury's are planning a store at East Huntingtower.

Livestock auctioneering was pioneered in Perth by an even older firm, Hay and Co., which operated from Dunkeld Road and then Methven Street, before moving to large premises in Victoria Street, known as the Victoria Mart.

This massive warehouse was one of the great icons of twentieth-century Perth. A branch line of the London and North-Eastern Railway can be seen in front of the building.

The firm moved, in 1918, to a more suitable location in Craigie, close to the railway, and finally closed in 1992. Both Macdonald Fraser and Hay and Co. were, in many ways, heirs to the great trysts at Crieff and later Falkirk, where huge droves of cattle, sheep and horses, in their tens of thousands, descended on these towns from the Highlands, as did buyers from all over Britain.

The railway also served the harbour area via a branch line from the south. Built in the 1850s, it extended as far as the Lime Shore and, in time, covered both sides of the harbour basin. One might have expected to find major industrial activity in a part of Perth served by both harbour and railway but, with the exception of Thomsons Dye Works and laundry, this never happened. The reason may have been the adverse effect that the railway had on harbour trade. In a communication with the Admiralty of 1865, concerning the proposed Tay Bridge, the Council drew attention to the fact that harbour trade had been prosperous until 1845 when competition with the railways – three years before they actually started operating in Perth – affected it to such a serious and permanent degree.

Small-scale industry abounded, though – such as Enoch Tomey's Tay Glass Works and, a century later, the Ysart Brothers' glassworks where the highly

An aerial view of 1947 showing the old Macdonald Fraser auction mart. Caledonian Road School can be seen in the centre of the photo, the Old High Street runs along the bottom, while Caledonian Road and Elibank Street (now demolished) lead towards the station.

collectable Vasart glass was made. A number of public utility buildings were also sited in this area – usually those that were not so desirable in the town centre. They included a smallpox hospital, the slaughterhouses, a new home for the dung depot (away from the Glasgow Road) and gas and electricity works.

Industry and commerce in Perth owed much to the harbour and the railway but the town has always had a large agricultural hinterland and this was reflected in other forms of trading activity. Today there is a clear-cut division between town and country but this is a relatively recent development and, indeed, before United Auctions moved to East Huntingtower, large animal

A view of Enoch Tomey's Tay Glass Works at the Shore. The men in the factory doorway appear to be glass blowers.

transporters were a common feature of the streets of Perth – as were, less frequently, animals which had escaped from the mart. Earlier in the twentieth century, sheep and cattle destined for sale were regularly herded into the city, either from surrounding farms or from holding pens on the outskirts.

The great fairs of Perth were noisy, celebratory occasions, bringing in people from the Highlands and elsewhere, where the animals and produce of the hinterland were sold, and where the townspeople enjoyed street entertainments – and also where fools could be quickly parted from their money and where drink-fuelled fights were, for some, the usual way of ending the day. The main fair of the year was the Midsummer Market, held in early July. Principally a horse and cattle market, there were, nevertheless, many other goods and entertainments on offer and the High Street was packed with stalls, all full of produce. The St John's Day Market, which, judging by its name, may have been pre-Reformation in origin, was held in early September and was also mainly a horse and cattle market though, in the earlier nineteenth century, it was also known for butter and cheese. Contemporary accounts describe how carts laden with dairy produce extended the whole length of George Street, down part of Charlotte Street and occupied the foot of the High Street. In

A stall in the High Street during the Little Dunning market of 1922.

earlier days, it was attended by many Highlanders who brought blankets, plaid and sheep to sell, the last-mentioned being bought by local butchers and kept on the North Inch until ready for slaughter. As this market clashed with one of the Falkirk trysts, the Perthshire Farming Society, which seems to have acted on behalf of local farmers in dealings with the Council, suggested, in 1814, that the fair be brought forward by a week to enable farmers and dealers to attend both. The Little Dunning Market, held in October, was the main feeing market of the year when farmers and farm workers gathered near the cross and agreed employment for the season ahead. The Andermass Fair was another horse and cattle market, held on the North Inch in early December, just after St Andrew's Day. It too may have been a survivor from pre-Reformation times. Of these fairs, the only remaining vestige is Midsummer Saturday, the start of the local trades fortnight. Little Dunning did not survive Word War II in any meaningful way and simply died away. The Andermass market had likewise faded from public memory until its recent revival.

Fairs apart, Perth had held markets from the earliest days, as is testified by references to the market place in the charter of c. 1210. Cattle were sold in a variety of locations, such as, in 1819, the west end of Canal Street which, at that time, was one of the main access roads to the Coal and Lime Shores and, therefore, already choked with horses and carts. In 1823, though, with the new gas works now occupying the site of the Canal Street market, the Council decreed that, henceforth, all cattle markets should be held on the eastern division of the South Inch. Thereafter, they seemed to switch on a fairly regular basis between the North and South Inches, depending on the level of protests from either side of the town. In 1847, for example, a petition from 77 cattle dealers and farmers on the north side complained about the inconvenience of having the weekly cattle market on the South Inch and of having to drive large numbers of cattle through the streets. They prayed the Council to grant them the use of the North Inch instead and their request was granted. A few months later, a petition to transfer the market back to the South Inch was refused. Again, in 1859, two rival petitions to the Council resulted in no change, though there was a growing public resentment that the wishes of a few farmers and cattle dealers to remain on the North Inch were overruling those of many townspeople. George Condie wrote on behalf of the latter, referring to the North Inch market as 'an annoyance to the residents and destructive to the amenity of this end of the town'. He further pointed out that access to the Inch was impossible until 2.00 p.m. on market day and that the grass and paths were dirty and strewn with hay. He then referred to the terms of the excambion with the Earl of Kinnoull (more of this in the following chapter) which stated that the Inch was to be kept solely for pleasurable purposes and not used for agriculture. The Council's response was to try to limit the market to the area between the back of Charlotte Street and the river. In 1864, in response to a proposed move back to the South Inch, the residents of Marshall Place petitioned the Council against it, saying they would be unable to bleach clothes on the Inch because the ground would be 'destroyed'. Finally, in 1867, the decision was made to move the market away from the Inches altogether, relocating it in an area by the river at the old Coal Shore.

As the nineteenth century progressed, with a growing middle class living in better housing in an expanding Perth and as sanitation and health improved, cattle were increasingly seen not as an essential part of the local economy but as an unhygienic and sometimes dangerous nuisance. In time, the cattle markets gave way to more modern methods of selling animals pioneered by firms like Macdonald Fraser and Hay, the straggling herds in the streets were replaced by road and rail transport and the annual Perth Show became the principal – and far more widely accepted – reason for bringing farm animals into the centre of Perth.

Closely connected with the cattle markets was the sale of meat. South

Street, prior to the construction of the flesh market, was the main area for this trade with burgesses selling from stalls and others, from the country, displaying meat on the backs of horses. But the unpleasant and messy business of slaughtering animals and preparing carcasses had to be regulated. (Fleshers were prevented from slaughtering near St John's Kirk in 1751.) and the Council, therefore, decided, in 1761, to build a flesh market on the bowling green at College Yard, the area now occupied by the City Hall. The market was open by 1765 and, to make sure that all fleshers now operated from it, their old stalls elsewhere in town were demolished. Those who persisted were prosecuted.

In terms of area, the flesh market at that time occupied more space than any building in Perth – more even than its close neighbour a few yards away, St John's Kirk. The interior courtyard was divided into northern and southern sections, the latter for members of the Flesher Incorporation and the other for the 'unfreemen' butchers in the town. The surrounding walls should have made it secure enough though incidents of dogs gaining entry and thieves breaking in resulted in the walls being heightened in the 1780s. By the early 1800s, there was a developing trend for butchers to revert to old habits and operate from outside the flesh market, forcing the Council to take action against them on at least two occasions. One of these butchers, an unfreeman, took advantage of the uncertainty over the precise boundaries of the royal burgh and opened a shop which he claimed was beyond the boundary and, therefore, beyond the jurisdiction of the Council – a claim they found difficult to disprove. By 1827, when so many butchers were openly flouting the old regulations and had opened shops all over the town, the Council decided to use the vacant space for housing several of the other markets in town. The butter market, which had previously been at the foot of the High Street, and poultry market had already been resited there in 1821 and they were now joined by vegetable dealers, kitchen gardeners, plant dealers and potato dealers. The meal market stood just outside the flesh market, on its eastern side. One major change of use was the building of the old City Hall over the west end of the market in the mid 1840s. Thereafter, following the dispersal of the various markets to other parts of town, the old flesh market premises seem to have fallen into disrepair through vandalism and neglect and were eventually cleared away.

Horse markets were also a feature of life in old Perth and seem to have been as unpopular with the public as those for cattle. In the earlier nineteenth century, the horse market occupied almost the whole length of South Street, before being confined to the area west of Princes Street, thus leaving the main road to the south clear. Later, though, it was held east of the Princes Street junction, an area busy with railway passengers going to and from the Princes

Street station and with residents walking between the town centre and the new residential areas to the south of the town. A petition of 1866, by residents of South Street, St John Street and Princes Street, gives a vivid picture of what the ensuing chaos was like. With dealers galloping horses along Princes Street and South Street, there were inevitably accidents and shopkeepers found they were losing business from a natural reluctance of shoppers to risk life and limb during the hours of the market. A further petition against the market resulted in new regulations. From 1868, it was confined to the area west of Fleshmarket Close, with the running of horses taking place behind barricades and on sand spread over the area to prevent them slipping on the cobbles.

The mercat cross in King Edward Street is one of the few visible references to the old markets of Perth. Dating from 1913, it is a reminder of the original cross which was both the civic and geographic centre of the old town, being situated where the two main medieval thoroughfares – the High Street and the line of Skinnergate and Kirkgate – met. Monarchs were proclaimed at this spot, local and national legislation was made public, the new year was welcomed and, presumably, it was also where the earliest markets were held. It was removed by Cromwell, as was much of old Perth, during the construction of his immense citadel on the South Inch, and rebuilt on the same spot in 1669. Council records show that it underwent occasional repairs, such as in 1728 when a new unicorn was commissioned. Its demolition was ordered in 1765 on account of the obstruction caused to carts and carriages and it was sold to a mason for £5 (it having cost £200 to build) who promptly knocked it down and removed the stone. The shaft survived, though, and has ended up in the grounds of Fingask Castle. The site of the cross is marked in the road and, despite its long absence, was still used for official announcements such as the proclamation of George V in 1910. Such ceremonial was transferred to the present mercat cross, the design of which is closely based on the previous one, complete with unicorn.

The success of the linen industry in the later eighteenth century spawned a number of offshoots, some of them surprising. Rags, for example, which could loosely be described as a textiles by-product, were essential for paper-making and their ready availability led to Perthshire becoming one of the centres of the Scottish paper industry. James Morison, a partner at one of the paper mills, came from the well-known Perth family of printers and publishers who would undoubtedly have benefited from what was presumably a cheap supply of paper. Printing may have begun in Perth as early as 1702, following the grant of £12 Scots to assist Daniel Gordon, a Dundee printer, to set up a printing house in the town. The money was also to compensate him for the loss of his type during a journey north from London. Whether or not he did actually establish himself in Perth is unknown as the earliest surviving example of printing in the town came off the printing press which had been sent to Perth during the 1715 Jacobite occupation for the purpose of issuing Jacobite proclamations. George Johnston set up a press in 1770 and, in his four brief years, produced a number of items such as the *Perth Magazine of Knowledge and Pleasure*. The mantle then fell on Robert Morison and his son, the above-mentioned James, whose prodigious output in the late eighteenth century – some 20,000 to 30,000 volumes per year – put Perth at the forefront of Scottish printing and publishing. The highpoint of publishing in the city was the *Encyclopaedia Perthensis*, a remarkable 23-volume work which was intended to rival the Edinburgh-published *Encyclopaedia Britannica*. The Morisons also founded one of Perth's principal newspapers, the *Perth Courier*, in 1809 and became printers to the University of St Andrews.

James Morison's son, David (whose lasting legacy was the design of the Pantheon-inspired frontage of Perth Museum and Art Gallery), invested in a business closely allied to printing – the manufacture of ink – and, in a further spin-off, the manufacture of bottles for ink is reckoned to have been the start of Perth's world-famous glass industry which culminated in John Moncrieff's glassworks. Developing an idea from rival glassmaker, Enoch Tomey, Moncrieff started producing industrial gauge glass which was in demand all over the globe. The firm also employed Barcelona-born Salvador Ysart who, together with his sons, created the art glass known as Monart from which Vasart ware later developed. Perth's reputation for glass was further enhanced by the opening in 1979 of Caithness Glass at Inveralmond, for whom Paul Ysart had later worked. John Moncrieff's business, the North British Glass Works, latterly known as Monax, closed in 1995. The site in St Catherine's Road is now used for housing and only the names of the new streets there – Monart Road and Vasart Court – bear witness to Perth's long and distinguished history of glassmaking which finally ended in 2008 with the closure of Caithness Glass.

Mention should be made of General Accident, a world-class insurance company which was founded in Perth in 1885 and maintained its headquarters in the city until it merged first with Commercial Union in 1998 and then with Norwich Union in 2000. Like the linen industry, it, too, could be said to have developed from Perth's agricultural hinterland. When legislation came into

OVERLEAF. *Some fine old buildings at the foot of the High Street, including the Scoon and Perth Masonic Lodge with its arched windows, were demolished to make way for the extension to General Accident's headquarters.*

An interior view of Wood's shop, stationers and booksellers, at 52 High Street, around 1900. The Bear's Kingdom *and other children's books are displayed on the table.*

force in 1880 making employers potentially liable for industrial accidents, a number of local businessmen, including some farmers, grouped together to provide themselves with insurance cover, and thus the GA was born. From its first office at 44 Tay Street, the company moved to the purpose-built premises (later much extended) on the south corner of Tay Street and High Street which now serve as the headquarters of Perth and Kinross Council.

Much business in Perth was done across the counters of the town's shops which, in the days before chain stores and supermarkets, were as unique to Perth as Dundee's were to Dundee. Some shopkeepers grew wealthy. Robert Brough and Robert Hay Robertson, for example, left money and paintings to form the nucleus of Perth's new art gallery but most were doubtless content to earn enough to keep food on the table and boots on the children's feet. Some too were proud enough to have their shops photographed and others were happy enough with shabby shopfronts, peeling paint and, probably, chaotic interiors. Most of the old town-centre shops succumbed in time to those big chains able to afford High Street business rates, though many will still remember High Street stalwarts such as Garvie and Syme the ironmongers, Norwells the shoe shop, Kennaways the bakers, Charles Rattray the tobacconist, Cairds the clothing retailers and Woods the bakers. With them have

St John's Square in 1985, just prior to demolition. The several Royal Burgh of Perth coats of arms at first-floor level were a measure of the civic pride in this shopping centre when it first opened.

gone the colourful shop awnings which sheltered the pavements on sunny days, the shop signs above doorways, the longer opening hours (and the Wednesday early closing) and a generally more relaxed approach to selling.

Retailing in Perth became more serious in the 1950s with first the introduction of American-style supermarket shopping and then the construction of St John's Square on land recently vacated by the clearance of the Meal Vennel slums. Completed in 1961 and occupying a large part of the area between Meal Vennel and King Edward Street, behind the High Street and South Street frontages, this was Perth's answer to the attractive but competing shopping developments of Dundee and Stirling. The style was contemporary and concrete, with pillars, arcades and grassy areas, and flats above the ground-level shops. The design, however, was flawed from the start as, while the first Marks & Spencer and the popular record shop, Concorde, ensured a lucrative footfall during the day, its silent and dark corners at night tended to attract the town's drunks and skinheads. The sixties' architecture, too, dated quickly and St John's Square was not greatly missed when, in 1985, the demolition men moved in. It has since been replaced by the St John's Centre shopping mall which, at the time of writing, has lasted almost as long as its predecessor and shows no signs of waning popularity.

CHAPTER 3

THE LOST STREETS AND OPEN SPACES OF PERTH

Perth began to outgrow its medieval boundaries only in the later eighteenth century. Until then, its expanding population, resulting in part from agricultural reform and clearances in the Highlands, was being squeezed ever more tightly into the area between Mill Street, Methven Street and Canal Street. Although a degree of cartographic licence can be observed in some early seventeenth-century maps, which show elaborate formal gardens behind street frontages, there was clearly a considerable amount of open space at that time. The rather more accurate maps of a century later show this space diminishing and, by 1900, it had virtually disappeared altogether. While the steady outward expansion of the Georgian and Victorian periods and later is well documented and readily observable, the infilling of the town centre is less so. Buildings – industrial, commercial and domestic – were crammed piecemeal into impossibly tight spaces, linked to the outside world by stairs, pends, vennels, closes and streets. A prime example of this trend was the construction of the first City Hall in the centre of town, whose size and somewhat irregular shape seem to have been dictated solely by the available space. Access to one of Perth's most important buildings was via a rundown part of the flesh market, later known as City Hall Square, and narrow vennels from High Street and South Street.

The main open spaces in Perth today are the North and South Inches, two ancient areas of parkland which, in a little over 200 years, have changed radically in appearance. One of the biggest changes to the North Inch was its virtual doubling in size, following an excambion – or exchange of ground – with the Earl of Kinnoull. First proposed in 1790, with a view to improving the racing on the Inch, the excambion was completed in 1803, giving the town some of the lands of Muirton and Balhousie in return for land in the Tullylumb and Unthank areas. As part of the exchange, the earl also stipulated that the Inch, when extended, should be kept solely as an area of parkland, neither to

There is so much of interest in this 1776 print of the North Inch – the new bridge, the old road to Dunkeld crossing the Inch, the cattle, the fishing nets and, at the bottom right, the bull pen. Courtesy of the AK Bell Library, Local Studies Department, Perth and Kinross Council

be built on nor ploughed. The line of the Balhousie lade was to be altered and the road to Muirton, which then passed through the middle of the Inch, was to be removed. Both the earl and the Council saw these measures as a way of preserving the Inch 'for the health and recreation of the inhabitants' and as a contribution to the civic improvements already underway. The following year, work was begun on levelling and embanking the new extension, as well as planting new trees and felling older ones. During 1805–06, the wall which extended from opposite Balhousie Castle in a north-easterly direction across the Inch and which marked the old boundary between the town lands and the lands of Muirton was removed. Known as the White Dyke, it had been built in around 1727 in order to keep Muirton farmers off town land and, according to tradition, was financed by fines levied on the town's brewers and bakers for fighting with the weavers. The Muirton Bulwark was the name given to the wall erected shortly after to mark the new boundary.

It is doubtful whether that laudable aim of preserving the Inch for the recreation of the inhabitants was achieved in those early days. The jurist and diarist Lord Cockburn, writing on a Sunday evening in April 1842, states:

I don't believe that there have been 100 persons, and certainly not 200, on the North Inch this *whole* day. It has been an utter solitude, in the morning, between the two public services, and even in the evening . . . That plain of green velvet on which the very sun seemed delighted to repose, edged by the silver Tay, and surrounded by all the appearances of vernal life in the finest condition; bounded towards the one end by distant blue mountains, some snow still lingering on their loftier summits; and towards the other, by the beautiful bridge, and its comfortable little city, ought to have been swarmed over by the young and the old, the cheerful and the pensive, but especially by the pious on this their day of thought, from the morning to the evening twilight.

The North Inch was Perth's back garden, used by the townspeople for a variety of occupational, as well as recreational, purposes. Linen cloth laid out on the North Inch for bleaching mirrored in a small way the commercial bleachfields around Perth in the eighteenth century. Only domestic bleaching was permitted, though – a regulation the townspeople had to be reminded of on several occasions. There were also poles for drying clothes which, together with the cloth laid out for bleaching, must have given the Inch every appearance of an industrial laundry. Watchers were appointed by the Council to combat the theft of washing left out overnight on the Inch.

Somewhat at odds with white linen and clean washing were the many cows which were allowed to graze on the Inch. Grassmail – the yearly rate payable to the tacksman of the Inches (he who leased the right from the Council to collect dues from those using them) by the owners of cattle – was 20 shillings per cow in 1801. The hours of grazing at that time were limited to between 4.00 and 8.00 in the morning and between 2.00 and 7.00 in the afternoon and evening, which limited the risk of over-grazing and allowed the washers and bleachers a bit of cow-free time. There were a few bulls too but they were provided by the tacksman and generally penned up in a stone enclosure at the top of the Inch. Under the terms of the tacksman's lease, they were not to be 'fierce or vicious' but, if, on occasion, they were found roaming free, the complaints were not slow in coming in.

Cowfeeders – who earned a small income from looking after cattle on behalf of butchers and others – had a difficult job, particularly as cattle during

OPPOSITE. *Clothes watcher Bob Sidey on the North Inch, washing billowing behind him and cloth bleaching in front. One wonders if the dog kennel had wheels too.*

the course of the nineteenth century were increasingly regarded as an urban nuisance. A lengthy dispute began in 1827 between the residents of Rose Terrace, one of the smartest areas of Perth, and the Council over the issue of whether or not cattle had a right of access to the Inch via that street. The residents drew attention to the regular soiling of the street and the health hazard to children playing, which, for most other areas of the town, was an accepted everyday state of affairs. Military exercises on the Inch, as well as galloping horsemen and players of quoits, football and golf, all drew complaints from the cowfeeders about their grazings being destroyed. Outbreaks of rinderpest and foot-and-mouth disease added to their difficulties. The Council finally put an end to the centuries-old custom of cattle grazing on the Inch as late as 1924, the only objectors being the Perth and District Dairymen's Association. They did, however, make a return during World War II.

The Rose Terrace objectors of 1827 were indicative of the growing trend to make the Inch an attractive rather than simply a utilitarian feature of Perth. This trend was further reflected in a report on the Inch's trees which recommended ornamental planting with species such as mossycup oaks, limes and poplars, all to be carefully positioned either to link in with earlier plantings or to soften the starkness of the back of Charlotte Street or even just to hide the bull pen. The many humps and hollows were gradually removed over a long period – a process which made county cricket, rugby and hockey possible in the twentieth century. Levelling had its critics, such as the town's skaters who used to make good use of the frozen hollows on the Inch – unless, to their annoyance, the ice had already been taken for the purpose of packing fish. A further indication of the North Inch's new respectability was the construction of the bandstand in July 1891. Those who complained of it being too far away – it was roughly opposite where Bells Sports Centre now stands – were condemned as non-music lovers by the *Perthshire Advertiser.* Nevertheless music lovers in their thousands turned out to watch the opening spectacle which featured the band of the 6th Dragoon Guards. The bandstand was gifted to the town by James F. Pullar, a younger son of John Pullar, and demolished in 1958 following concerns over its safety.

The South Inch had a history similar to that of the North. It too was increased in size, thanks to an excambion with the King James VI Hospital and the gift of land by the Glover Incorporation, one of the town's eight trade associations. In Marshall Place, it had a row of prestigious housing bordering one side and there was a similar prohibition against building on the Inch or at least within 400 yards of Marshall Place. Clothes were hung out to dry on washing lines strung between trees (unlike the North Inch where there were poles for

The bandstand on the North Inch was presented to the town by James F. Pullar in 1891.
This photograph was taken no later than 1903.

this purpose) and were guarded by clothes watchers. And trees were either planted or removed to improve its appearance – for example, either by hiding the lime sheds or by exposing the attractive housing at St Leonard's Bank.

It differed, though, in its proximity to the shore and its eastern edge was frequently disfigured by ships' cargoes, such as wood, coal and stone, being dumped on the grassland, where, of course, they were prone to theft. Other parts of the Inch were blighted by dung hills and later, in the 1860s, by the poles and wires of two telegraph companies – all of which would have paled into insignificance had the plans to house the General Station on the Inch been brought to fruition.

At some considerable distance to the west of Perth, though belonging to the town, lay a large expanse of land known as the Burgh Muir. Several times larger than the old town itself, its spaces were used for a variety of purposes, ranging from executions and cattle markets to the Midsummer Fair. The timber shortages of the eighteenth century, caused by the constant demand for fuel and building materials, presumably lay behind a description of the Burgh Muir in 1714 as 'barren and almost fruitless'. This prompted the Council to undertake a mass planting of 14,000 firs in that year, which was followed by further planting and even a brief and unsuccessful search for that source of power and fuel so constantly in demand, coal. By around 1747, at the time of General Roy's *Military Survey*, the Burgh Muir was so heavily wooded that avenues had been cut through the trees, radiating out from a central point. It was named as Perth Wood on a map of 1792 and some of the avenues at that time (different from those in 1747) have been preserved in the layout of the streets of the Viewlands area today, such as Muirend Road which was labelled on the 1792 map as the Great Avenue. Today, several street names in this area hark back to its forested past. Sales of wood provided a useful source of income for the town but, perhaps as a result of many trees having been destroyed in a storm in 1791, the Council decided to clear much, if not all, of the Burgh Muir the following year and then began a lengthy debate about the future use of the land. In the early 1800s, decisions were taken to auction it off in feus, with some of them to be turned into farms and some to be used for villas. While such auctions were advertised as far afield as Edinburgh, they also appealed to wealthier locals and successful bidders included bookseller James Morison. The decision seems to have been beneficial to the Council as, by the 1830s – all the lots having been disposed of by 1828 – it was bringing in several hundred pounds in feu duty each year. The transformation of the Burgh Muir was described in 1836 by George Penny who wrote that the whole of the wood had been cleared and 'was studded with gentlemen's houses and tradesmen's neat cottages'. The 'barren and fruitless' land of 1714 was now remarkably fertile, producing some of the county's best crops of wheat and barley.

The main access roads to the Burgh Muir had been via the Old High Street and Dovecotland and by the road known as the Burgh Muir Loaning, which extended westwards from Kinnoull Causeway and then followed the line of what is now Viewlands Road. A small section of it can still be seen running between Glover Street and Glasgow Road. Modern roads are now plentiful in the once silent and wooded Burgh Muir, servicing the housing that began to cover it from the later nineteenth century onwards.

On the east side of the river and south of today's Bowerswell Road, much of the lower slopes of Kinnoull Hill were occupied by the Perth Nurseries.

Established in around 1766 by James Dickson, a scion of a well-known Roxburghshire family of horticulturalists, they expanded to occupy around 60 acres of land. By the 1840s, and at that time employing around 80 people, the firm had developed into one of the best-known plant nurseries in Britain, if not wider afield. The claim that they supplied much of Perth and Perthshire, and large areas of Scotland, with trees and shrubs is substantiated by a stock check of the later 1800s which apparently recorded around ten million trees actually in the nurseries. The customer base was huge and embraced all parts of the country and all levels of society, including the then Duke of York who was organising the planting of Windsor Great Park. As well as trees and shrubs, the nurseries supplied flowers and vegetables and were one of the first firms in Scotland to deal in swedes, the seeds having been sent to Perth from Sweden by the great Linnaeus himself. Rather more fragrantly, the Scots rose was also propagated there. In time James Dickson was succeeded in the business by his brother William who, on his death in 1835, left both the nurseries and his home at Bellwood to his nephew, Archibald Turnbull. Bellwood survives but no longer in the splendid isolation of former times – the nurseries were feued out by the Earl of Kinnoull in the later nineteenth century and are now occupied by large villas and generally upmarket housing. They have sizeable gardens, though, with some fine old trees still growing there, which may indeed be the last vestiges of this once renowned business. The name Dickson and Turnbull survived until the 1990s in a little shop in Hospital Street, though few visiting it would ever have guessed the firm's long and distinguished history.

Another large area of open land appears on maps of the mid nineteenth century as the Patriotic Gardens. They were established by the Patriotic Society in around 1850 to provide the working classes with allotments, in the belief that the cultivation of land encouraged habits of temperance, religion and morality. The gardens, which covered a large area behind the street frontages of Newrow, the Old High Street and County Place, were particularly popular with the residents of Dovecotland as the land they had been using hitherto was in the process of being taken over for the new Wellshill Cemetery. The allotments west of Caledonian Road lasted until 1875 when they were bought by Macdonald Fraser for redevelopment as a livestock auction mart, while those to the east survived a little longer.

Smaller pockets of land, often with intriguing names, were found all over the city, most of them now built over. Horse Cross, perhaps the best known nowadays on account of its association with the new concert hall, was formerly an open area adjacent to Castlegable which derived its name from the town's carriers who used to gather there with their horses and carts. The Cow

A view of the south-eastern end of Castlegable in 1922, with the open area of Horse Cross on the right.

Causeway lands were purchased by the town in 1747 and are now where the AK Bell Library and County Place are situated. They were laid out partly as orchards and leased to a tacksman of the town who would, presumably, have endeavoured to make an income from the sale of fruit. Later they were used in part as a brickfield where hundreds of thousands of bricks were turned out. The Soutarlands, purchased in 1710, were formerly gardens before being partly covered over by the station. The Bow Butts, where archery was practised in the days of James I, was on the south side of the Old High Street, near the junction with Caledonian Road. The How Rig was a low-lying, marshy strip of land on the south side of Canal Street, between today's Princes Street and Scott Street. It was a popular spot for skating when it froze in winter. Corbs Croft, purchased in 1756 and later proposed as the site for a new artillery barracks, was just to the east of the Gibraltar Quay and where the Norie Miller Riverside Walk now is. The lands of Drumhar, bordering the lade at the north-west of the town and seemingly laid out as gardens in the later eighteenth century, were owned by the Council and leased to the government in 1794 as a site for a new barracks. The name is remembered in the Drumhar Health Centre and in the street names there. Maggie's Park was situated by the southern wall of the barracks and was sold by the town to the Baker Incorporation in 1834. It was once proposed as a burial ground for horses – not perhaps a natural bedfellow for the nearby cistern which supplied the town with drinking water. Depending on the position of the apostrophe, one horse at least was presumably buried at Cuddie's (or Cuddies') Grave which can be found on the outskirts of the city on the road to Scone. Those stout four-legged workers who hauled the first trams in and around Perth and Scone were rested there. The site was once occupied by the Bridgend waterworks and is now laid out as a garden. Clayholes was on the south side of Long Causeway immedi-ately to the east of the railway line and, as the name suggests, comprised at least one pit. The area was developed for housing in the later eighteenth century and initially occupied by weavers. The Deadland, so named because it is believed to have been the site of a late medieval paupers' burial ground (and as such was outwith the town wall which followed the original line of George Inn Lane), was more familiarly known as the Diddledan and comprised that area of land which lay very approximately between George Inn Lane and the river, extending as far west as the Skinnergate. Before the bridge and George Street were built it was, of course, quite flat. The Deadland was purchased by the town in 1742 (though later acquired by Sir John Stewart-Richardson of Pitfour who, several times, offered it back to the town – unsuccessfully – in exchange for other property) and, in its time, played host to an orchard and gardens, a bowling green and a ladeside harbour for small pleasure boats, as well as a rubbish dump, industrial buildings and public lavatories. There was also an old footpath there, known as the Lady Walk, which provided access to the North Inch from the foot of the High Street, by way of a little arched bridge over the lade and, after 1771, the dry arch of Perth Bridge.

The Diddledan eventually disappeared when Tay Street was created and was but one of several streets, vennels and passageways which have been lost to Perth and in many cases to living memory. Slum clearance was the impetus behind the demolition of a number of streets in the earlier twentieth century and these are still remembered by some of Perth's more senior residents. A very few may recall Thimblerow, a narrow street accessed from a pend in the Old High Street, which was demolished in the 1920s. Though the tenements have gone, the character and speech of the residents have survived in a compilation of newspaper articles published as *Sandy McNab: or the Kronickles of Thummle Raw*. Written in Scots and probably not by anyone called Sandy McNab, the book consists of short humorous stories about life in the poorer quarters of Perth in late Victorian times. Parallel to Thimblerow on the east was Paul Street which, together with nearby West Mill Street, was built in around 1790. West of Thimblerow and close to the municipal boundary was Claypotts Wynd. Its location gave rise in 1863 to a complaint from residents about the town crier, who had formerly cried at Thimblerow and Claypotts Wynd but was now finishing his round at Paul Street. The residents asked the Council to remind the crier that they were within the royal burgh (the boundary was not always clear, as we have seen) and that he should perform his royal burghal duties properly. Since the demolition of this area, much of it is now occupied by car parks and by Caledonian Road.

Castlegable ran from the north end of Skinnergate in a north-westerly direction to North Port and was demolished in around 1930, along with the north side of Bridge Lane. It was once a well-populated street and busy with travellers from the north who would have entered the town at the North Port before proceeding along Castlegable and Skinnergate to the High Street. Nowadays, instead of being condemned as a slum and demolished, the housing there would perhaps have been modernised and the street prettified, forming with the Fair Maid's House a quaint corner of old Perth, but, as it was, the extension to the museum, opened in 1935, filled the space.

Pomarium, a name which derives from the orchards belonging to the medieval Carthusian monastery in the area, was built in the later eighteenth century and comprised a long row of terraced houses, running north to south and virtually parallel with King Street which lay a little to the east. Known as the Pow or Powmarry in the local vernacular, it was occupied mainly by handloom weavers in the early nineteenth century and, as their financial fortunes dwindled, mainly owing to the advent of mechanisation, so, it seems, did the street. The houses were eventually demolished in the 1950s and replaced with Perth's first multistorey block of flats.

Commercial Street, in its latter years, was a sleepy and poor part of Bridgend and ripe for demolition in the 1970s – a far cry from the days of the pre-1621 bridges when it had once been the main approach to Perth from

OPPOSITE. *Looking from George Street down Bridge Lane, with the road to the left leading to Skinnergate and Mill Street and the vennel on the right to Castlegable. This was taken in 1933 when the only remaining tramlines were those in George Street.*

Dundee and Blairgowrie. Its decline and neglect was a direct consequence of the opening of the present Perth Bridge and Gowrie Street which took away all through traffic. Perth Civic Trust made a brave attempt to prevent its demolition and, while many may mourn the passing of yet another part of old Perth, few would dispute the success of the housing which now occupies the site.

While Perth residents are familiar with the tree-lined Edinburgh Road which cuts through the South Inch, they may be surprised to learn that a similar one crossed the North Inch, starting at North Port and heading towards Muirton and Dunkeld. It was formed in around 1738, some 30 years before the present Edinburgh Road, and lasted until around 1803 when its removal was made one of the conditions of the excambion with the Earl of Kinnoull. By this time, though, the main route to Dunkeld already followed the line of today's Dunkeld Road which suggests that the road across the Inch was probably little used.

One of Perth's most historic streets, dating from medieval times, survived until the mid 1980s before disappearing beneath the St John's Centre shopping mall. Meal Vennel, which together with Watergate once provided the only vehicular access between High Street and South Street, derived its name from the girnals or meal stores which were to be found there. Many of the vennel's substandard but characterful old stone buildings were cleared away in the 1950s and replaced with brick and concrete back entrances to the shops of the St John's Square shopping development. In the 1980s, the Civic Trust argued vociferously that Meal Vennel, even in its drab state, should not be allowed to disappear for good but to no avail. All that remains of this ancient street are small signs in shops indicating its former whereabouts. Quite possibly leading off Meal Vennel in the direction of the town kirk was the ancient Argyll Gate which is recorded as having an east–west alignment. However, it disappeared so long ago that no trace of its location survives.

Meal Vennel was a wider and more significant thoroughfare than most surviving vennels in Perth today and, as such, was sometimes simply known as The Vennel. The word vennel is believed to derive from the French *venelle*, meaning 'a lane or passageway', and is one of several examples of the linguistic link between Scots and French. From studying the old maps of Perth, it would seem that a vennel was generally open at both ends, while a close, as the name

OPPOSITE. *Looking north along the straight and narrow street of Pomarium in around 1930. It originally led from Newrow to the South Inch before the railway blocked its southern end.*

Meal Vennel in around 1930. The entrance to Central District School was at the right of the photograph.

OPPOSITE. *Albert Close in the 1930s with what purports to be the last remaining section of the old town wall. Sources suggest – and old maps seem to confirm – that the end of this close joined at right angles with another leading from the High Street, past the former entrance to the Ship Inn.*

suggests, was open at only one. This is not entirely accurate as Kirk Close leads from the High Street to St John's Place, though the very fact of its crooked, dog-leg shape suggests that perhaps it began as a close and a through route was made at a later date. A similar example is provided by Albert Close which, today, is a short, straight passageway between George Street and Skinnergate but, in the nineteenth century, had two right-angle bends, suggesting that two or even three closes had been knocked into one.

There were, and indeed still are, several other vennels in the town. Some, such as Fish Vennel by the river, which was latterly known as Glen Close, have disappeared for good, some are now unnamed and others, perhaps thought to

be lost, are merely masquerading under alternative names. The last-mentioned category includes Masterson's Vennel, Mickle Vennel, Cumming's Vennel and Duff's Close which are now respectively Cutlog Vennel, Water Vennel, Oliphant's Vennel, and Fleshers Vennel. In a triple name change, St Ann's Vennel became School Vennel, so named because of the nearby old Grammar School, and has since reverted to St Ann's Lane. This gives the lie to the natural assumption that streets and street names must be equally old. Rather, it seems, they acquired, probably through common usage, names that reflected a feature of that street. Candlemakers Close, for example, was named from the nineteenth-century candle works there and Albert Close, formerly Barret's Close, took its name from the nearby Albert Inn.

The disappearance of Salt Vennel resulted from an excess of traffic in the town. The Council minutes of 1791 describe how an increase in trade led to more activity at the harbour and more people coming into Perth from the country. Those coming from the south added to the traffic from the harbour going north, all using the one street, Watergate. Greyfriars burial ground, however, was to the south of the town and funeral parties from the north all went the opposite way along Watergate, resulting in a chaotic confusion of too many carts and carriages trying to avoid each other. To relieve the situation, the Council had, for a while, been considering creating a new street between High Street and South Street, passing on the east side of St John's Kirk, and, when the opportunity arose to buy a ruined tenement at the south end of Salt Vennel, on the line of the proposed new street, the Council made a successful offer. By 1795, several other properties had been both purchased and demolished and, by the following year, the new thoroughfare had been named St John Street. By this stage, though, it only extended from South Street as far as the church and then turned to the west as far as Kirkgate. It was only in 1801 that the St John Street we know today was fully open.

There were rather more closes in the town than vennels and, in many cases, their names, if not the actual closes themselves, have been long forgotten. Several obviously derived from personal names, such as Kennedy's Close, Graham's Close and Gordon's Close, all off South Street, while others were indicative of nearby activities, such as Shuttlefield Close (off Canal Street) and Fleshmarket Close (leading to the flesh market from South Street). Some too derived from pub names, such as White Bull Close (off the High Street), and others from significant buildings, such as Guild Hall Close (off the High Street) and Chapel Close (off the Old High Street). This last-mentioned category includes the medieval Parliament Close which now lies under the present Marks & Spencer. It was home to an ancient building, Parliament

Shuttlefield Close, probably during demolition in the 1870s as part of the scheme to extend Scott Street from its junction with Canal Street northwards to South Street.

House, which was believed to have been where the Scottish Parliament met on occasions, up to the seventeenth century, and, while no proof of this exists, there is at least some circumstantial evidence in its favour. Parliament House was later home to the qualifying Episcopal congregation in the eighteenth century before it fell into disrepair and, in 1818, was finally demolished. Several of the above-mentioned closes disappeared in the last quarter of the nineteenth century as part of the city improvement schemes which included the creation of King Edward Street, the extension of Scott Street (already existing between Marshall Place and Canal Street) through to South Street in around 1877, and later to the High Street, and the extension of Kinnoull Street from Mill Street through to the High Street.

The streets, as we have seen in the case of Watergate, were busy and probably much busier than they are today. With the vast mass of the growing population still living within the bounds of the old medieval town, in unhealthily overcrowded conditions, and with little by way of home entertainment, there was no incentive to stay indoors and thus the play and recreation areas for children were the town's streets. And, notwithstanding the high mortality rate for under-fives, there were a great many children – according to the 1861 census, for example, a total of 82, aged between five and nine inclusive, lived in Watergate, an already busy thoroughfare even without hordes of playing youngsters. For the great majority of adults too, the street, if not the public house, was the natural meeting place for the exchange of news and gossip.

The streets were also full of animals – household dogs and cats scavenged for scraps, horses hauled carts and carriages or were ridden proudly by the military, cattle were driven by cowfeeders to and from the Inches a couple of times a day and farm animals were herded from nearby farms either to market or to the slaughterhouses. So great was the congestion in Perth on market days that, in 1796, the Council devised an early one-way system. All cattle droves entering the town by way of the bridge and heading west, south or north were required to use the main outer roads rather than attempting to enter the main central area. Horses were stabled at various points around the town, including at many inns. The town's stables, built in 1761 on part of the remaining earthworks of Cromwell's citadel, were a response to the expensive problem of the town having to find stabling for horses belonging to the military. They were thus primarily for military use and survived until 1802. A popular spot for watering horses, known simply as Horse Water or the horse watering place, was at the riverside on the North Inch, a little above Perth Bridge. Hay was brought into the town for feeding animals and was generally weighed out and sold at the town's stillyards. One was erected on the South Inch in 1779 but this soon led to complaints from neighbouring farmers and townspeople about the inconvenience of hay carts filling the streets in the autumn of each year. Another was erected in 1792 on the North Inch, thus allowing farmers from the Kinnoull side of the river to enter Perth by way of the bridge and proceed directly to the North Inch without having to go through the town. As with other branches of the town's revenue, the right to the income from the still-yards was auctioned off to the highest bidder.

Well-fed animals in town contributed to the sanitation problems already caused by the lack of a proper means of disposing of human waste. George Penny, writing in 1836, describes what it had been like:

> Besides the inconveniences arising from want of light at night, the streets during the day were in a most deplorable plight with filth. At all hours the contents of dunghills, etc., were wheeled out on the streets, and there left, perhaps until next day, waiting the conven-ience of the farmers to drive them away. Every housewife emptied her soil-buckets whenever she took a fancy, so that the streets exhibited a most unseemly appearance. From morning to night the celebrated metropolitan custom of 'Gar-de-loo' was universally practised: hence it was no uncommon thing for a person to be overwhelmed with a deluge of this abomination. The streets got a kind of a sweep by a few worn-out old men, who were quite incapable of performing their duty with effect.

The first serious attempt to improve sanitation in Perth was set in motion by the passing through parliament in 1811 of the town's Paving, Lighting and Cleansing Act. This first devolution of powers from the Town Council to a separate body with fund-raising powers arose from the Council's inability to afford the mushrooming costs of looking after the town's streets. The new act provided for the appointment of commissioners with the authority to raise money from the inhabitants in order to pave, illuminate and clean the streets, as well as for the establishment of local police and fire services. The amendment act of 1819 even required householders to rail in flowerpots on windowsills.

Despite the setting up of this new body, generally known as the Paving Commissioners, the disposal of dung remained a contentious issue for a long time. That which was removed from the streets had generally been taken by cart to the South Inch and dumped, lying there sometimes for long periods until it was bought for some small sum by local farmers. In times of food shortage, though, such as during the wars with France in the early nineteenth century, farmers were prepared to pay high prices for dung – so high, in fact, that it was financially worthwhile to import it from London. By 1818, the 'dung stances' had been removed from the South Inch to Tullylumb, perhaps urged by the middle classes of Marshall Place who expected something rather more fragrant wafting through their expensive windows. Tullylumb was initially at a suitable distance from the town though, as housing began to expand westwards and as the railway companies began to need more land in that area, it once again became a difficult issue. By 1854, the Scottish Central Railway was complaining about the smell and the serious nuisance being caused to passengers and railway staff and were joined in protest by almost 200 residents of York Place who were similarly affected. By 1890 and with the poorhouse having been built close by, the Board of Supervision, which supervised the administration of the Poor Law, declared the dung depot (as it was then known) illegal. A new depot was finally opened at the shore in 1898, just to the south of the new gas works, and presumably survived until made redundant by motorised transport and the removal of cattle from the streets. It is now the home of the Friarton Recycling Centre.

Narrow streets laid out in medieval times were increasingly a hindrance to an expanding population. The Skinnergate, one of the town's oldest streets, was not only one of the narrowest but, up to the late eighteenth century, one of the main entries to the town from the north. Many of the old houses in this street had forestairs – external open stairs providing access to the upper floors. However, they jutted into the street and, in 1734, the Council took steps to have them demolished, offering compensation to the owners. Those in the Watergate were removed in the 1760s and others followed in the early nineteenth century under powers delegated to the Paving Commissioners. The straightening of streets was also being carried out at this time, not necessarily as part of street widening, although this often coincided, but more with a view to making the streets more attractive in appearance. In this age of enlight-enment, the appearance of the town was becoming more of a consideration than hitherto. From a detailed examination of old maps, one can see how crooked corners were straightened and how protruding buildings were remod-elled or rebuilt in line with others in the neighbourhood. In 1845, for example, the Council persuaded the proprietor of a tavern and stables on the east side of North Methven Street to give up some street frontage in order to align that part of the street with other properties.

One of the most important of such projects was the widening of Perth Bridge. Although greatly admired when first opened in 1771, it was criticised very early on for its narrowness and was, indeed, at times, dangerous – and, occasionally, fatal – for pedestrians when meeting with 'much infuriated' oxen. Proposals to widen it were hampered from the beginning by the problem of getting a quorum of Bridge Commissioners. The original commissioners consisted of, amongst others, anyone who contributed to the building costs by lending the sum of £200 sterling or donating 20 guineas. Around 50 benefactors fell into this category, including several peers and the Archbishop of York – whose elder brother, the 9th Earl of Kinnoull, just happened to be the prime mover behind the construction of the bridge. As commissionership in the case of Perth Bridge was hereditary in the male line, the job of tracking down a sufficient number of commissioners to make a quorum at any given moment was almost impossible. Indeed, this inability of the commissioners to take decisions about even basic repairs was having a deleterious effect on the bridge's fabric. Nevertheless, after much talk of widening and even an abortive attempt to buy a second-hand footpath formerly attached to the redundant Stockwell Bridge in Glasgow, work finally began in 1869. The old stone parapets were removed, iron brackets were attached to the side of the bridge, new pavements were laid on both sides and a new metal parapet was erected. The work was finished in early 1870, the cost having been met by public subscription and a highly successful fund-raising bazaar – so successful, in fact, that the surplus was put towards the proposed City Hall organ, that which now resides in Melbourne, Australia. The improvements were not universally popular as some felt the beauty of the original structure had been marred and others thought they were unnecessary, the railway having considerably reduced the amount of traffic crossing the bridge.

Pavements were widened too but at the expense of the roadway. In 1874, traders in the High Street complained about the recent reduction of the carriageway which allowed barely enough room for a horse and carriage to turn. So bad was the resulting congestion on Friday market days, with carriages, carts, goods displayed on the streets and people, that the police had to direct traffic to avoid potential accidents.

Carriages and carts have, of course, disappeared from the streets of Perth, the internal combustion engine having put an end to horse-drawn vehicles, but it was a slow death and there will be some alive today who still remember them. Carts, ubiquitous, were in constant use for the everyday transport of goods, both within the town and beyond. In the mid nineteenth century, Perth was served by over 80 carriers who took loads on specified days of the week to all parts of Scotland and even to the major English cities such as London, Liverpool and Manchester. Carriages were used by those who could afford them. A taxi trip by carriage from Bridgend to the General Station in 1895 cost one shilling and sixpence, compared with tuppence on the tram. Carriages,

OVERLEAF. *A horse-drawn coal cart, with a little girl trotting barefoot behind, turns into High Street from South Methven Street.*

however, were not permitted on the North Inch, a Council ruling which led to an unfortunate spat with the Earl of Kinnoull. The dispute blew up in 1863 over the earl's wish to be able to drive his carriage to his Balhousie Castle front door via the path around the Inch, a not unreasonable request for the period considering his and his family's beneficence towards the town. However, when the Council objected and when the earl, perhaps provocatively, increased to carriage-width the access to the castle from the Inch, the Council responded by placing posts in front of the opening, thus preventing the passage of any wheeled vehicle. The earl died less than three years later and the Council were quick to praise him as a good friend of Perth as, indeed, he had been.

Stagecoaches and mail coaches quickly fell victim to the railway in the late 1840s, the only survivors being coaches serving Highland Perthshire, such as *The Queen of Beauty* (a lovely name redolent of the owner's pride) and the mail coach to Inverness which ran until the later 1850s when that town was linked to the south by means of the railway line to Aberdeen. Just prior to their demise, Perth was linked to the rest of Scotland by the following, all leaving from either the Salutation Hotel or the George Hotel and calling at the other a few minutes later: the *Defiance* (a four-horse coach which left for Aberdeen at noon); the *Duke of Wellington* (to Inverness at 6.00 a.m.); the *Atholl* (to Blair Atholl at 4.00 p.m.); the *Defiance* (another one, it seems, this time to Blairgowrie at 4.30 p.m.); the *Real Champion* (to Dundee at 7.00 a.m.); the *Fair Maid* (to Dundee at 4.00 p.m.); the *Tally Ho!* (to Edinburgh at 6.45 a.m., via Falkland and Kirkcaldy); the *Saxe Cobourg* (to Edinburgh at 9.15 a.m., via Kinross and Queensferry); the *Defiance* (yet another, to Edinburgh at 1.45 p.m., via Kinross and Queensferry); the *Victor* (to Glasgow at 5.45 a.m., via Crieff, Dunblane and Stirling); and a fourth *Defiance* (a four-horse coach to Glasgow leaving at 4.00 p.m., via Auchterarder, Blackford and Stirling). Independently of these, and with a terminus near the Salutation Hotel, was the *Wonder Coach* which left for Dundee at 7.00 a.m., returning later in the day. In terms somewhat reminiscent of a certain youthful local bus company in the early 1980s, which just happened to be called Stagecoach, they advertised 'low fares as were never before offered to the public'. There were also several mail coaches running at the same time, to the same destinations.

For much of the nineteenth century coaches – and, indeed, all travellers – would have had to pass through turnpike barriers which were lifted on payment of a toll. Royal Mail coaches and those on foot were exempt but most others had to pay. Money was collected at the toll houses on the outskirts of Perth. Some have survived such as those on the Dundee and Edinburgh roads but others have been demolished, even in relatively recent times. The unautho-

There are signs and notices everywhere in this interior view of the General Station but perhaps the most surprising in that age of coal and steam is one banning smoking.

rised removal of the Dunkeld Road toll house near Muirton in 1967 incurred the wrath of the newly formed Perth Civic Trust which had been on the point of making a detailed photographic record of it but at least the perpetrators, a formerly well-known local bus company, had the grace to apologise. In contrast, the demolition of the Crieff Road toll house in 1997 was welcomed by the many who had come to regard it as an eyesore.

The railway in Perth, which so quickly brought to an end the old and (to us) romantic days of stagecoach travel, has altered significantly since its heyday in the earlier twentieth century. The main lines, radiating north, south, east and west from the General Station, are much as they were in the railway's earliest days though Perth's position as one of the country's main railway centres – when it was once described as a 'railway inferno' at certain times of the year – has long since been lost. The cuts from the 1960s onwards have meant the closure of carriage and wagon workshops, the axing of major services such as the motorail link with London, the abandonment and sale of the once vast and technologically advanced marshalling yards and, of course, the loss of hundreds of jobs. All this has been mirrored in the public face of the railway at Perth, for the General Station, once one of the more impressive examples of British railway architecture, now looks as ordinary as it once was grand. The station was built in the late 1840s and, when viewed from Marshall Place or Leonard Street, presented an imposing 180-metre-long frontage, complete with a Tudor-style octagonal tower and an awning over the main entrance. It was much extended and altered in the mid 1880s, the main addition being the long curving platform of the 'Dundee Station' which served trains to and from that city. It was connected to the General Station by footbridges. The present station entrance, built in the later twentieth century, has moved the focus of attention away from the old facade while the car park in front – like some of the nineteenth-century improvements – obscures it even more.

The Princes Street station, to which the Council reluctantly acquiesced in return for the Dundee and Perth Railway renouncing its claim to build on the South Inch, was opened in 1849 (though the buildings followed a few years later) and, with its sidings, grew to occupy the whole area between the water-works and Princes Street, south of the railway line itself. The ground had to be built up to reach the level of both the railway bridge and the General Station which, for passengers, meant a climb up a long flight of steps from Princes Street. Its proposed closure in 1965 angered a number of railway passengers, including staff of McEwens department store who argued that they would have to take a train a whole hour earlier to get to work on time. This, however, cut no ice with the railway authorities who were well used to brickbats flying in after the Beeching cuts and they closed the station in 1966. The land was bought by the Council in 1984 and subsequently developed as flats known as The Archery.

For a brief two-year period, there was also a station at Barnhill which served as the Perth terminus for the Dundee and Perth Railway. In reality, it

An early view of the imposing frontage of the General Station. Were it not for the awning and the signs beneath it, the building could almost be taken for a row of town houses and a church. Courtesy of the AK Bell Library, Local Studies Department, Perth and Kinross Council

OVERLEAF. *Members of the Guildry Incorporation at Princes Street station in around 1890.*

was not so much a new station as a conversion of the old Barnhill House which, owing to its close proximity to the new railway line, was purchased by the railway company for that purpose. The station closed when the railway bridge and the new Princes Street station were opened and the site is now occupied by the small Island View estate, accessed from the Dundee Road.

The severe pruning of the railway network in the 1960s was partly a result of the development and growing popularity of other modes of transport – the lorry, bus, private car and even the aeroplane. One of the first local bus

A horse-drawn bus heavily laden and on the point of departure from Scone to Perth.

services was the brainchild of a Mr Greenfield of Scone who, in 1863, formed a limited company, bought horses and a bus with a capacity for 31 passengers and hired a driver. He operated primarily between Scone and the General Station, for which he charged a fare of 4d for sitting inside and 3d for sitting outside. He also ran a less frequent service from Balbeggie to Perth. The success of the service can be measured in the passenger statistics for the 16-month period between 1894, when the bus company was taken over by the newly formed Perth and District Tramways Company, and September 1895, when tram services commenced. The buses in this period carried a total of over 167,000 passengers, which, very approximately, equates to around 400 per day.

The horse-drawn trams provided a relatively fast service, covering the initial route between Scone and the Glasgow Road terminus in only 30 minutes. In time, the network extended to Cherrybank, Craigie and the Dunkeld Road while electrification in 1905 resulted in an even faster service and a number of horses with P45s. The first accident, a collision between a

A horse-drawn tram at Priory Place in Craigie around the turn of the twentieth century.

tramcar and a potato cart, occurred in the first week of service and may have augured troubled times to come for, although the trams were popular, the Council (which took over the service at some considerable cost in 1903) found it almost impossible to make any money from them. After long years of trying, the Council finally withdrew the trams in 1929, yielding to pressure from new motorised bus services. The old tramlines were dug up shortly after (though they could still be seen at the entrance to the former Scone terminus until recently), leaving, as the only visible sign of their existence, a few metal brackets attached to buildings (such as those in George Street) which supported the overhead cables.

With cars and buses in the ascendancy, few would have thought, in 1929, that they too would all but disappear from the town centre. They were, though, a victim of their own success as traffic congestion, for which Perth was infamous in the post-war years, led to the construction of the by-pass and the creation of the inner ring road system and, in time, the restoration of peace to the pedestrianised High Street and St John Street.

CHAPTER 4

THE BUILDINGS OF LOST PERTH

Many of Perth's public buildings owed their existence to the social, medical and technological advances of the nineteenth century, as well as Perth's growing conception of itself as not just a town but a city. A prime example is the City Hall. The present hall, lying due west of St John's Kirk, has lain empty for several years pending a decision about its future and is the second to occupy that site. The earlier hall was first proposed at a Council meeting in February 1844 as a response to the lack of a large hall for public meetings in the town. Churches had hitherto allowed their buildings to be used for such meetings but there was growing disquiet about their use for gatherings of a particularly secular or political nature. With remarkable speed, the Council, in April, approved the proposal to build a new hall over the western part of the virtually redundant flesh market and, by January 1845, the hall had been formally opened. And not opened once, it seems, but twice. The Council was divided over the most suitable way to mark the occasion, with one faction arguing for a fashionable soirée to raise funds for the infirmary and the other for a 'public civic evening banquet' of wine, cake and music for the inhabitants and public bodies of Perth. The latter held sway, one shilling and sixpence being the admission fee for 'grown people' and one shilling for those aged 14 and under. The other faction, however, not to be outdone, arranged their own opening soirée for a few evenings later, complete with the same musicians.

The hall, as mentioned above, was hemmed in by surrounding buildings, resulting in both a pedestrian appearance from the outside and a lack of natural light inside. But plenty of gas lighting was installed and roof lights added a degree of natural illumination, although they had to be protected by wire from stone-throwing vandals. Externally, the proximity of the market was an additional problem in that evening visitors had to thread their way past potato carts to gain access.

Numerous organisations made full use of the hall, which quickly took its place at the heart of life in Perth. All had to pay for the gas consumed and almost all had to pay a hire charge though charitable organisations, such as the Perth Total Abstinence Society, and those which were for 'the general improvement of the community' were offered a reduced rate. Farmers belonging to the Perth Corn Exchange Association paid an annual sum for the use of the hall on Fridays between 11.00 a.m. and 3.00 p.m., strictly on the understanding that it was not to be used for hiring farm servants. The recently founded Perth Choral Union had the use of the hall on Friday evenings in 1862. So successful had it been in its stated purpose of fostering 'musical taste in the community' that a large hall was needed to cope with its rapidly increasing membership. Art appreciation, too, was fostered by way of several art exhibitions and the display of paintings belonging to the Literary and Antiquarian Society which had been presented to them by the Marquess of Breadalbane. Including portraits by local painter Thomas Duncan and other works by old masters such as Caravaggio and Giordano (or so it was believed at the time), they hung in the hall from 1847 until 1884, when they were returned to the society – complete with holes and other damage caused by fire and condensation. Improving lectures were held but none by Charles Bradlaugh, the militant atheist, who was refused permission to use the hall in 1879 and who, the following year, as a newly elected MP, would cause a commotion in parliament over the oath of allegiance. An appeal was submitted on the grounds of free speech and that the hall should be for public purposes of all kinds but it was rejected almost unanimously. And bazaars were regularly held, in aid of the Conservatives, the Liberals and many other local societies and good causes.

The hall was also used for major civic events such as Freedom of the City conferrals. Several of these occasions were hastily organised when it became apparent that a possible candidate was to be passing through the town. Many famous names from nineteenth-century history passed across the City Hall stage to receive their burgess tickets, including Lord Palmerston in 1853, Lord Rosebery in 1898 and Andrew Carnegie in 1902. The Council had more trouble with Gladstone who was offered the freedom on no less than three occasions and, while he professed his grateful thanks for the honour, he was just too busy to come and accept it. He was finally cornered in 1879. On 10 March 1863, the wedding day of the future Edward VII, after festivities and rejoicings throughout the town, a banquet was held in the hall for 300 inhabitants, complete with a choir (presumably the Choral Union) and the band of the Perthshire Militia.

Lord Randolph Churchill made two memorable speaking visits to Perth. During the first, in 1889, he gave what was described as the best speech ever heard in the City Hall. This photo is probably of the aftermath of the second occasion when, in April 1893, he spoke against Irish home rule to a combined audience of 8,000. Unionist slogans adorn the balcony and the Union Jack covers the table on the stage.

Some rentals backfired. After the militia had used it in 1856, the Council had to spend a considerable sum in drying and airing the hall, clearing drains, painting and replacing window glass. The military featured again in 1875 when Captain Pearson of the Perthshire Rifle Volunteers wrote to the Council saying that they had been looking for a drill hall for some time and wondered if they would consider selling them the City Hall. The Council did, indeed, consider and resolved not to sell but instead to raise a public subscription with a view to re-roofing and generally improving it. Perhaps the speed of building in 1844 was to blame for its poor condition a mere 30 years later. Shortly after their offer was rejected, the Volunteers built a drill hall near the waterworks in Tay Street.

The City Hall was under threat again in 1879 when plans were announced for a new, privately funded public hall on a plot of land in Tay Street between the drill (or Volunteer) hall and Canal Street. This proposal seems to have been a response to the need for a decent hall for public entertainment in Perth, as the design of the City Hall was not ideal for spectator events. The Council took the view that such a scheme endangered the future of the City Hall, and engaged the city architect, Andrew Heiton, to undertake a survey and make recommendations for its improvement. And it wasn't happy reading for the Council. The roof was difficult to keep watertight, the 16 cast-iron columns supporting it obstructed the floor space and impeded the view of the platform, the ceiling was too low for the size of the hall, ventilation was poor and heating inadequate. Despite the cost, though, at least some of the proposed work was carried out over the next few years.

By 1904 and with the financial repercussions of the collapse of the grand-stand on the North Inch the previous year probably much in mind, the Council was growing increasingly concerned not just about the City Hall's appearance and shortcomings but about its safety. Built to hold around 1,800 people but with an insufficiency of doors, there was an awareness that any serious accident occurring when the hall was full could be a potential disaster. In such a situation, as they well appreciated, the cost of compensation could be many times that of building a new hall. Once again the Council was divided. The *Perthshire Courier* described how one faction sought to improve the exits and give the hall a facelift while the other argued for the demolition of an old building 'in a tumble-down condition' and starting anew. The latter cause was aided by a partial collapse of the ceiling during the annual lifeboat service in 1907. The congregation panicked and disaster was only averted by a quick-thinking choirmaster who launched his singers into a stirring rendition of the 'Hallelujah Chorus', thus immediately reassuring the gathering – either that or they thought they had already entered the Pearly Gates. The debate swung both ways over a period of time but the decision was eventually taken in 1908 to build a new City Hall. The final event in the old hall was an entertainment given by W. F. Frame on 2 May of that year.

The new City Hall opened in 1911, closed in 2005 and, at the time of writing, is scheduled for demolition. It may not be the city's most attractive building and it may, indeed, detract from the view of St John's Kirk but, while it stands, it represents the high level of civic pride in Perth at that time – pride in a city whose exports were known over the globe and pride in a city which had been making remarkable improvements in a number of fields.For many local people the hall has been the backdrop to their lives, for it has hosted a wide range of events over the years, from concerts, classical and pop, to

The second City Hall, with attractive gardens in front, served the Perth public between its opening in 1911 and closure in 2005. This photograph was taken in the 1930s

sporting and political gatherings, and from coffee mornings and jumble sales to school choirs performing at the Perthshire Musical Festival. Indeed, some local people owe their very existence to the hall, their parents having first met at one of its regular Saturday night dances.

Perth's first hospital in the modern medical sense was not, in fact, the King James VI Hospital, the funds of which were devoted rather more to the care of the poor, but the County and City of Perth Infirmary in York Place (now the AK Bell Library). Immediately prior to its foundation, the physicians and surgeons of Perth had provided a service to the inhabitants from their own 'shops' in town and also provided medical assistance to the poor through the Perth Dispensary which was founded in 1819. It was staffed by a team of eight local doctors who took it in turns to dispense both advice and medicines, inoculate against cowpox and pay for midwives to attend expectant mothers. A long-term wish was the provision of an infirmary where those suffering from fever could be isolated from other family members, thus minimising the risk of further infection. Fever wards had been set up on a piecemeal basis, usually in the middle of serious outbreaks of infectious disease, but were not universally popular amongst the well. In 1825, for example, when the Council approved the temporary conversion of rooms in the Session House to fever and surgical wards, free of charge because it was for the public good, the objections of the town's reverend gentlemen about the risk of infection to them prompted the removal of these wards to another building instead. In late 1831, when cholera prevention schemes were being drawn up, the Council even approached the Lord Advocate to seek permission to use the hospital of the Depot (now Perth Prison) as a fever ward. The infirmary proper thus originated in the urgent need to provide a permanent and sufficiently large fever ward, capable of dealing with outbreaks of cholera, and in the bequests of the Earl of Breadalbane and of local physician, Dr Patrick Brown, who left £3,000 and £500 respectively to go towards the foundation of the same. Within a few years, and doubtless spurred on by the relentless advance of cholera at that time, a total of £6,000 had been raised and work had begun on the new infirmary. It was designed by the city architect, William Macdonald Mackenzie, whose name is carved on the entrance arch to what is now the library. Three years after its opening, George Penny, in his survey of Perth in 1841, stated that 'this splendid institution has already been of immense benefit to the middling and lower classes of the community. There has [sic] already been 43 operations performed successfully, some of them of a very dangerous description.' It was an immensely important advance in local health care, not merely for the reason given by David Peacock that 'no public receptacle for the diseased, nor for the treatment of sudden and violent injuries, [had] previously existed in the county', but for the pressure directed at the Council by hospital management to improve both public health and the cleanliness of the town.

By the end of the century, the infirmary was struggling to cope with the pressure of its own success – success that had been crowned in 1888 with the queen's approval of the 'Royal' prefix to mark her jubilee. When an outbreak of scarlet fever in 1899 filled the infirmary to overflowing and resulted in patients having to be treated in the smallpox hospital at the shore instead, the Council began a long debate on whether to rebuild the ageing hospital on its existing York Place site or build afresh elsewhere. They eventually opted for the latter

OVERLEAF. *A men's ward at the old County and City of Perth Royal Infirmary in York Place. Biblical texts and a new year's greeting decorate the walls. Two nurses stand in the background.*

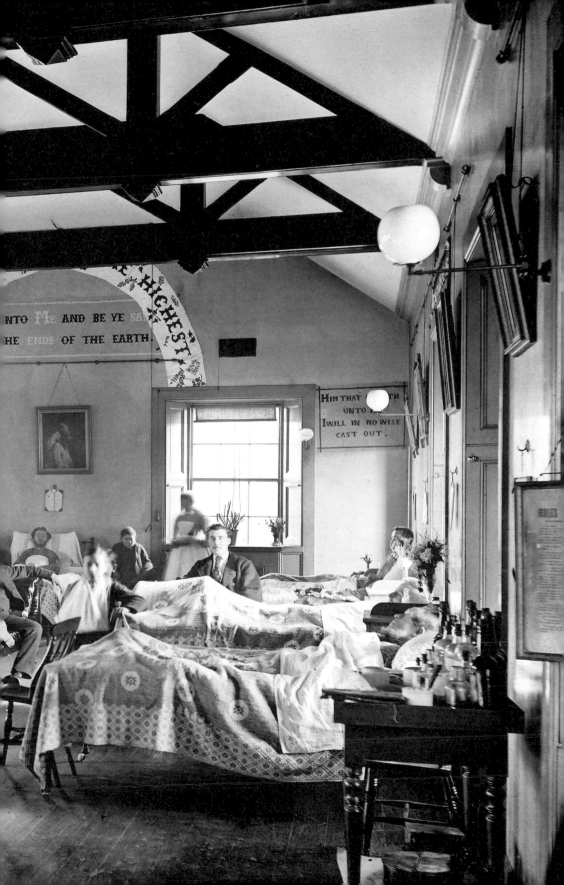

and the new County and City of Perth Royal Infirmary opened in 1914 on a site at Tullylumb acquired from the Glover Incorporation. The old infirmary thereafter was resurrected briefly as a wartime Voluntary Aid Detachment (VAD) hospital before being sold to the Perthshire Education Authority in 1920. Much extended and with a completely redesigned interior, it reopened as the AK Bell Library in 1994.

The development of smallpox vaccine in the eighteenth century provided a measure of defence against another dread disease of the period. Following a major outbreak in 1860 which infected 700 townspeople and took the lives of 60, several hundred residents each year took advantage of the opportunity to be vaccinated. The reluctance of many, however, who chose not to take this step – perhaps because of a natural suspicion of the whole procedure (the cost of 3d per vaccination is unlikely to have been a significant deterrent) – allowed the disease to retain a foothold in the city. The Police Commissioners, in 1876, considered building a separate smallpox hospital but rejected the idea on the grounds that the infirmary was intended for sufferers from all diseases. Within ten years, though, they had changed their minds and a small hospital for smallpox patients was built on what was then an isolated site at the shore. It survived as such until the 1930s and has since found another use.

Perth's two fever hospitals, whose purpose – apart from relieving pressure on the infirmary – was to isolate patients from the community, were similarly built at the edge of town. Both town and county authorities erected hospitals for their own patients, the town choosing a site at Friarton, where a complex of red-brick buildings, complete with the royal burgh's coat of arms, was completed in 1906. The county opened theirs some years earlier, in 1900, on a site at Hillend. When the development of antibiotics made fever hospitals virtually redundant, they too were adapted to new uses. The Friarton hospital was incorporated into the Friarton Prison complex in the early 1960s, while the other became the Burghmuir Hospital for the care of geriatrics. It closed in 1981 and was demolished shortly after, to be replaced by Beechgrove House, a residential care home.

The Society for the Relief of Incurables in Perth and Perthshire, whose aim was to provide care for the long-term chronically sick who could not be nursed at home, was launched in December 1875 with a successful fund-raising bazaar. With almost £1600 in the bank, they began looking for a building to act as a small hospital but, with Nimbyism alive and well in Perth even in those days, it was an almost impossible job. As the first annual report pointed out, they did not wish to force themselves into places where they would be unwelcome, even if the objections were based 'on an unreasonable prejudice'.

Their first hospital opened in the old Kinnoull schoolhouse (now a dental surgery) in October 1876, the building having been vacated when the present Kinnoull School, erected by the Perth School Board, opened earlier that year. They mainly admitted patients from the infirmary and, with a total of five beds, were proud to think of themselves as a large family, rather than a hospital. The hospital scale, though, if not atmosphere, arrived in April 1883 when the society took over Hillside, a private dwelling between the Dundee Road and the river, and enlarged and altered it to suit their needs.

Serving as an annexe to Hillside was the Barnhill Sanatorium, set in several acres of grounds higher up the slopes of Kinnoull. Funded by Sir Robert and Lady Pullar, it was opened in 1901 for the care of tuberculosis sufferers who benefited from its airy verandahs and well-ventilated accommodation. Tuberculosis – or consumption – had a dreadful mortality rate, carrying off annually well over 2,000 people at the turn of the twentieth century in Glasgow alone and several such sanatoriums were being opened at this time across the country. In 1948, both Hillside and the sanatorium were brought under the wing of the National Health Service. At this time, though, major advances in the treatment of the disease permitted many patients to be treated at home and thus, with the need for a sanatorium much reduced, it closed in 1958 and was partially demolished before being converted into a private home. Hillside Homes continued until 1997 when the poor state of the buildings necessitated its closure and subsequent demolition.

The poor formed a sizeable proportion of the town's inhabitants and, in the absence of a welfare state, were generally looked after by a number of different organisations, including the Council, the Incorporated Trades, the Kirk Sessions of the town's churches, benevolent individuals and numerous charities. In 1832, for example, at the celebrations to mark the passing of the Reform Act, the Council gave bread, cheese, porter and a small sum of money to around 2,000 of the town's poor, which equated to around 10 per cent of the population. The following year, the minister of the East Church argued for better heating in his church so that, amongst others, 'the poor, who are often rendered uncomfortable at home by means of cold, should be enabled to look to the Church as a place where they may experience both bodily and spiritual comfort'. There were seats in church and schools for the poor, medical assistance from the doctors of the Perth Dispensary, charities for the distribution of coal and other basic essentials, job creation schemes, the Perth Soup Kitchen which, in 1859, provided almost 200 daily servings of broth and rolls to the poor and hungry of Perth and even burial places for the poor. Descriptions of the royal wedding celebrations of 1863 illustrate the various classes of poor in

Perth which included the inmates of the poorhouse, who were given a substantial dinner, the 'outdoor poor' (those still in their own homes rather than the homeless) who were given a shilling each to provide themselves with the same and the poor attached to the King James VI Hospital, around 70, who were given half a crown.

A number of poorhouses were founded in Scotland following the Poor Law (Scotland) Act of 1845. The Perth Parochial Board was reluctant to shoulder such an expense without at least considering alternatives and thought about taking over the King James VI Hospital which, they argued, was virtually a poorhouse in all but name. When the Board of Supervision in Edinburgh dismissed the idea on the grounds of insufficient recreational space around it, the Parochial Board took over a lodging house in Cutlog Vennel instead (later the site of the Evangelical Union Church and more recently Perth Theatre). Running it as a poorhouse, they provided food, fuel, clothing, baths and a recreational garden for 80 individuals ranging from infants to bedridden nonagenarians, all supervised by an overseer and matron. This still left a good number of the destitute out on the streets and the provision of a purpose-built poorhouse could not be delayed much longer. It was finally completed in 1861, to a design of Andrew Heiton, on a site at the western side of the Glasgow Road and Glover Street junction. This was rather too close to the dung depot for the liking of the Board of Supervision who requested that the depot be moved elsewhere. It eventually was but only after the passage of almost 40 years.

An attempt was made, in around 1925, to modify the image of the poorhouse by renaming it the Bertha Home. Even so and long after it had ceased to be a poorhouse and was instead providing residential care for the elderly, many ageing Perth folk would have done almost anything to avoid going into the Bertha Home, such was the stigma of its past role. After World War II, the high prison-like walls surrounding it were removed and the ground fronting the Glasgow Road was laid out as a garden. In 1956, the Council, who had assumed responsibility for the building in 1930, tackled the problem of its image and, having rejected as an alternative name the Catherine Glover Eventide Home, opted instead for Rosslyn House, borrowing that name from Rosslyn Place, the row of houses on the opposite side of the Glasgow Road. The building was later used as local authority office space and has, more recently, been converted into flats.

The public baths were particularly appreciated by the poor. They were funded by public subscription, following a general meeting of the community in around 1845, and initially proposed for an area near the flesh market where it was thought the custodian of the City Hall could superintend both. In the event, they were built on a site over the lade between Methven Street and Kinnoull Street, where the (recently closed) public lavatories are today. The lade had to be arched over before building could begin but, together with water from the town's cistern at Maggie's Park, still provided sufficient water, hot and cold, to supply 13 bathrooms, four of which were exclusively for female use. There were also cold plunge pools and showers. Dr Malcolm, one of the town's physicians, who was 'conversant with the system and extent of public baths adopted on the Continent', advised on the construction which was completed and opened in 1846. Statistics show that, in 1847, a total of 7,457 baths were taken and, although it was a popular and socially useful institution, the bathing statistics did not always show an upward trend. In 1853, for example, the managers noted both a significant drop in use by the working classes and, perhaps not surprisingly, in those taking third-class cold baths. In the late 1850s, the baths were extended to include a wash house, the need for which may have arisen from the steadily growing population and the covering over of the lade which made public access to a plentiful supply of water increasingly difficult. By the early 1880s, the directors of the baths were in a quandary. Despite limited funds, they were faced with demands from the public for larger premises, hotter water and a public swimming pool, as well as the threat of legal action from the nearby North Church over smoke from their chimney. In the end, the height of the chimney was increased and a new boiler installed but the swimming pool, proposed for the vacant site immediately to the west, was built on the Dunkeld Road instead.

The demand for larger premises continued until 1905 when a large donation from Sir Robert and Lady Pullar allowed a new wash house, or steamie, to be built in Canal Street on land formerly occupied by the old gas works. Containing 48 stalls for washing, each with two tubs, a boiler and a clothes horse, plus wringers and blanket washing facilities, it was a functional if plain addition to the public buildings of the town – 'in keeping with the practical nature of the institution' was the phrase used in the press to describe the design. It was modern, though, being lit by electricity, which was perhaps a little odd bearing in mind the previous use of the site. This highly popular facility was doubled in size in the early 1950s at which time the Mill Street premises were finally demolished. The proposed demolition of the Canal Street wash house in 1966 resulted in a much publicised campaign to keep it open, led by Councillor Jean Hamilton – or Steamie Jeanie, as she was known. This resulted in a replacement wash house being built in 1973, adjacent to the old one, but, at a time when washing machines in the home were commonplace, it began to lose money and was closed in 1976.

Building work at the City Mills in 1918 uncovered some of the town's original eighteenth-century wooden water pipes, which once led from a nearby cistern to wells around the centre.

The even more important issue of drinking water was a continual problem for the Council over many years. The first attempt at a piped supply dates from around 1762 when the Council accepted an estimate of £150 to build a cistern at Maggie's Park, lay wooden pipes using trees from the Burgh Muir and channel water through them to 11 access points in the town. Water was to be diverted into the cistern from the lade at a point upstream of the town's mills. The scheme was extended in 1765 to include a supply to Newrow, Watergate and South Street, as well as to the flesh market. Lead pipes were introduced in 1786 but the technique of pipe laying was seemingly not sufficiently understood as, in 1797, in response to complaints about a frequently interrupted supply, the Council decided to get in touch with 'a man of science' who could advise them on laying pipes properly.

The suitability of lade water was severely compromised in 1794 by the construction of the barracks just a little upstream of the cistern's intake. Its occupation by hundreds of soldiers, all using the lade for their ablutions, compelled the Council to bypass the barracks by placing the cistern further upstream, complete with an elementary filtration system, but they also actively considered alternative water sources such as the springs at St Magdalene's Hill, Huntingtower, Kinnoull and those in the Burgh Muir area. By the early nineteenth century, the town's water supply was less than adequate, as was demonstrated by a petition from the inhabitants about poor water quality. The reason for this was made clear in a report of 1815 which revealed that mud and silt were blocking some pipes and others, particularly the remaining wooden ones, were full of holes.

Adam Anderson then appeared on the scene. Rector of the Academy since 1809 and with a background in chemistry, he submitted to the Council, in 1819, an analysis of the water from the Clathymore spring at Tibbermore which showed it to be a good and clean supply. The spring was over 70 metres above pavement level at Rose Terrace and supplied almost 1.5 million litres per day. The plan, however, was dropped when it dried up in dry weather and instead – for the first time, it seems – Anderson considered using water from the Tay. Finally, in 1829, after even the Guildry had offered to take over the task of supplying 'good water' to the town, the Council succeeded in gaining an act of parliament 'for supplying the city of Perth, and suburbs, and vicinity thereof, with water'. Adam Anderson worked closely with the newly appointed Water Commissioners, drawing up plans for the new waterworks and deciding on their location. A site near Greyfriars burial ground had originally been proposed but Anderson had it moved instead to the south-east corner of the woodyards, on the site of a chapel for seamen (today the corner of Tay Street and Marshall Place), on the grounds that the 'water that oozes from the burying ground' might come into contact with water pipes that may not be properly sealed. He pointed out that 'malicious or whimsical persons might have it in their power to agitate the public mind . . . with the most revolting reports respecting the quality of water.'

The waterworks were in operation by 1832, taking water from the Tay, filtering it and pumping it through the streets of Perth to public wells. By the middle of the century, many families had a water supply to their own homes, even to the upper floors, a luxury which put such a strain on the waterworks (originally designed to provide only street wells) that wider-diameter water pipes had to be relaid in the 1860s. The waterworks continued in operation until 1965 when new premises were opened at Gowans Terrace. The old building was saved from demolition by Perth Civic Trust and is now home to the Fergusson Gallery.

It is of no great surprise that the Council should have entrusted the design and engineering of the waterworks to a schoolmaster when one considers that the said schoolmaster had already successfully designed the town's gas works.

The old gas works in Scott Street in 1901. This photograph appeared in the booklet published to mark the opening of the new gas works at Friarton in that same year. Courtesy of the AK Bell Library, Local Studies Department, Perth and Kinross Council

Serving as what would now be termed a technical director of the Perth Gas Light Company, founded in 1822, Anderson supervised the design and construction of the new gas works which occupied the block bounded by Canal Street, Scott Street, Charles Street and Victoria Street – an area which was formerly a cattle market. Above the Canal Street entrance was placed an epigram by Horace – *Non fumum ex fulgore, sed ex fumo dare lucem* – which summarised the function of the gas works as primarily to produce light from smoke rather than smoke from flame. This was presumably the work of Anderson who, shortly before he died, was known to have written a similar Latin phrase above the entrance to the waterworks. By the summer of 1823, the Council had given the company permission to dig up the streets in order to lay gas pipes for street lighting, on condition that no more than 30 metres were dug up at any one time and that trenches were to be fenced off as well as lit at night and watched. In October of the following year, the first streets and buildings were lit by gas and much of the town quickly followed. It was stated in 1841 by

George Penny that 'a great proportion of the houses and almost all the shops are lighted with gas which is allowed to be the best in Scotland' and, indeed, there are early references in the local press to the 'peculiar brightness of Perth gas'. Despite these fulsome endorsements and perhaps because of the high prices being charged, the Perth New Gas Light Company started up in 1844 with a gas works lying between Curfew Row and Blackfriars Wynd (roughly where the Kinnoull Street multistorey car park is today). By 1845, the new company was busy digging up the streets and laying pipes and competing successfully for business, winning a contract in that year to supply a number of public buildings, including the Academy and the City Hall. The old and new companies amalgamated in 1868 and, three years later, were taken into public ownership under the management of the Gas Commissioners. They, in turn, ceded their powers in 1901 to the Town Council which ran the gas works until nationalisation in 1949. The ever-increasing demand for gas in the later nineteenth century necessitated enlargements of the gas works and finally, in 1901, the erection of a new gas works at Friarton. The two old gas works, never ornaments to the town, were quickly demolished once they had outlived their usefulness. The Blackfriars premises were sold to Pullars in 1874 while, as mentioned above, the site of the original Canal Street works was used for Perth's new wash house, Sir Robert Pullar's gift to the women of Perth.

The most visible sign – in every sense of the word – of Perth's new reliance on gas was the improved lighting of the town's streets. The first attempt at street lighting dated from 1746 when the Council erected smoky, oil-burning crusie lamps which gave off little more than a faint glimmer of light, certainly not enough to deter would-be thieves and robbers lurking in dark closes. By 1779, there were around 110 such lamps in the town, lit and maintained by coppersmith Pat Bisset for £85 per annum. In around 1782, the old crusies were retired and replaced with more efficient globe lamps, still fuelled by oil, though the glass globes were sometimes an irresistible temptation to the town's vandals. Bisset too was replaced in 1789 following his refusal, possibly with justification, to light the lamps during the hours of moonlight. Those successful in winning contracts to light the town's lamps tended to come from Dundee or Edinburgh, ports where whale oil was readily available for bulk purchase. In 1807, Smith and Stevenson from Edinburgh, in bidding to renew their contract, offered to trim and maintain the lamps at a rate of eight and half pence per lamp per week, as long as the price of the best Greenland whale oil averaged £30 sterling per ton in the Leith market, otherwise their fees would rise or fall according to the market price. Gas lighting was introduced in the mid 1820s and by 1841 there were a total of 238 gas street lamps throughout the town. Electric lighting came in almost immediately after the opening of the electricity generating station at the shore in 1901, though the last gas street light was extinguished as late as the 1960s. Both the red-brick generating station and red-brick gas works at Friarton are still standing, at least in part, and have found other uses.

Gas was a significant addition to a town already full of fire hazards arising from thatched roofs, narrow streets, candles, open fires, readily available alcohol and, in earlier times, the unregulated storage of gunpowder in shops and homes. The Council took a number of preventative measures over the years such as in 1751 when, presumably in the wake of a major fire, they bought a new fire engine, repaired the old one and prohibited the construction of timber tenements. Later, thatched roofs were also prohibited. Early fire services were rudimentary in the extreme – not only was the engine house in such poor condition in 1815 that it was difficult to get the fire engines out but the engines themselves were unreliable with reports of pipes bursting and fumbling efforts at repairs while buildings burned. The engines were maintained by the town's keeper of fire engines who reported, in 1819, that replacements were required. The Council, having studied details of those available for purchase from Hopwood and Tilley in London and considered the rate of water discharge and pressure and, of course, the price, agreed to buy one more engine and again raised the hope that insurance companies might make a contribution towards the cost, they standing to benefit as much as anyone. The Dundee Assurance Office had already donated one engine 'which had come to hand' in 1794 and, some years later, the County and City of Perth Fire Insurance Company agreed to finance another.

By 1826, the engine house was situated at the foot of South Street, in the vicinity of County Buildings. The three fire engines, one yellow, one blue and one 'small', were to be manned by two firemen each who were paid a retainer of one guinea per annum, plus a payment of one shilling per hour during the day, doubled at night, during call-outs. Keys to the engine house were kept by magistrates, the superintendent of fire engines and the jailer, though only the first two could authorise their use.

In 1834, the engine house was moved to the foot of the High Street, near the Council House, and, the following year, there appears a detailed report in the Council minutes about the state of the fire service. While the fire engines, they reckoned, were amongst the best in the country, this was of little use if the firemen themselves were little more than 'a self-willed mob' ignorant of how they should be used. 'It is well known that when a fire occurs the multitude are collected together in a state of great alarm and then all is hurry, bustle and

The men of Perth Fire Brigade stand proudly beside their engines outside the fire station in King Edward Street which bears the royal burgh's coat of arms.

confusion; everyone would command and each must have his own way of proceeding and thus mischief is often done to the engines and much time lost.' When a fire broke out in Newrow, the report mentioned three young men who 'were actually struggling on the roof of the house for who should hold the director while water was flying in the air producing no effect'. The report recommended that 20 properly trained firemen be retained, that they undergo regular refresher courses and be paid three shillings for the first hour of a fire, earning an extra shilling if they arrived within 15 minutes of the alarm being given. They were docked a shilling, though, if they arrived drunk.

From around 1850, the Police Commissioners were responsible for the fire service which now occupied premises in Tay Street, conveniently close to the police office at the foot of the High Street. The service did not enjoy a good reputation locally, with both men and machines being accused of underperforming, of which no finer illustration can exist than the destruction by fire of the Municipal Buildings on the corner of High Street and Tay Street in 1895, despite the fire station being virtually next door and the river just yards away. (To be fair, those who discovered the blaze assumed it to be a chimney fire and wasted valuable time by sending for the sweep rather than the fire brigade.) By 1922, however, as a fully professional fire service serving both town and county, their standing had substantially improved thanks to the provision of two state-of-the-art fire engines gifted by Miss Rachael Pennycuick and a brand-new fire station in King Edward Street. The fire service moved to Long Causeway in 1971 and the former red sandstone fire station was demolished in the early 1980s to make way for a department store.

Even less speedy than the fire service of old was the postal service and many were the complaints in the days of the mail coach, pre-railway, about delays to the mail north of Edinburgh. The post office in the later eighteenth century was on the corner of High Street and Watergate, from where it moved at some point to 80 George Street, virtually on the corner with Charlotte Street in a building which has seen several reincarnations as restaurants in recent years. It remained at this location for the greater part of the nineteenth century. Charles Sidey ran a stationery business from these premises as well as the post office and was succeeded as postmaster in 1819 by his son, Charles Graham Sidey, who also served as lord provost in the 1840s. Described in the *Perthsire Courier*, prior to its closure in 1862, as 'a miserable hole', the post office was replaced in that year with brand-new and significantly larger premises at the foot of the High Street, on the southern corner with Tay Street. There had been no masonic ritual at the laying of the foundation stone the previous year, perhaps for the reason that it was a public building, an omission which prompted the press to remark mournfully, 'We have seen a good dinner got up upon a much more flimsy pretext.'

The new post office received its share of complaints. No clock, said the press, and no external street lamp either which might have assisted visitors in avoiding 'nuisances' left by others. The staff were also a grumpy bunch, as can be assumed by efforts made in a newspaper to defend their civility: 'It is a perfect wonder if one can preserve his temper . . . So many absurd questions are put . . .' Despite the apparent size of the building, it too was turning into 'a miserable hole'. With a staff of well over 200 in 1894, some of whom had to work in sheds outside, the cramped accommodation necessitated a further move in 1898 to a prestigious new post office further up the High Street on the corner of what was then known as New Scott Street. Francis Norie Miller, the boss of the relatively young General Accident, had often coveted the High Street–Tay Street corner site and purchased it for his new headquarters when the post office moved out. Many will remember with affection the High Street–

Perth's post office occupied the corner of High Street and Tay Street between 1862 and 1898, before being replaced by General Accident's headquarters.

Scott Street post office, with its imposing soot-blackened exterior and dark interior with wooden floors and polished counters, all of which added a certain gravitas to that area of the High Street until it too was demolished in around 1973.

A number of significant private dwellings have also been lost to Perth, none more so than the Gowrie House which, for fame and size, was unmatched by any other private building in the town. However, because of its later use as a military barracks, it will be discussed more fully in a following chapter. There were, though, several other prestigious private properties in the town which served a similar function – that of providing a town house for the landed gentry and aristocracy while away from their estates. One such was the

town house of George Hay, first Earl of Kinnoull and Lord Chancellor of Scotland. This house, known as the Kinnoull Lodging, stood on the northern corner of Watergate and Water Vennel – the site is still vacant – and would once have been adjacent to the Gowrie House. It latterly served as a store for a nearby pub and was demolished in 1966, an act which was one of the spurs to the founding of the Perth Civic Trust the following year. Several other town houses were situated on the eastern side of Watergate which, despite its present appearance, was once a busy and fashionable part of town. Proprietors displayed proud coats of arms to the busy street and, on the other side, enjoyed the relative peace of gardens fronting the Tay.

Several large private houses were built on the Kinnoull side of the river, some enjoying river frontage and others enjoying a more elevated situation higher up the slopes. Of those that have been demolished perhaps the principal one was Tayside which stood in the Isla Road. Dating from at least the earliest years of the nineteenth century and quite possibly before, it was bought in 1870 by Robert Pullar who considerably enlarged it. It was later the home of another Pullars' boss, Frank Eastman, and then acquired by General Accident as additional office space. Following the completion of the final extension to their headquarters at the foot of the High Street in 1958, the General Accident staff moved back across the river and, three years later, the company sought planning permission to demolish Tayside and replace it with a futuristic office block. Ambitious plans for a ten-storey building were thankfully modified into a concrete and glass two-storey block which was later converted into a nursing home.

Also fronting the river but almost in the shadow of Perth Bridge was Bridgend House, famed for its association with John Ruskin, one of the intellectual giants of the nineteenth century. The house was owned by Ruskin's uncle, Patrick Richardson, and the young John spent many happy days there. He described it in his autobiographical work, *Praeterita*, as follows: 'My aunt who gave me cold mutton on Sundays was my father's sister: she lived at Bridge-end, in the town of Perth, and had a garden full of gooseberry-bushes, sloping down to the Tay, with a door opening to the water, which ran past it, clear-brown over the pebbles three or four feet deep; swift-eddying, – an infinite thing for a child to look into.' The house later bore a plaque testifying to the Ruskin connection, similar to the one still displayed in Rose Terrace,

OPPOSITE. *This post office on the corner of High Street and Scott Street served Perth for the greater part of the twentieth century. It was probably assumed that buildings of a similar height and grandeur would be erected beside it.*

The town house of the Earl of Kinnoull, Lord Chancellor of Scotland in the early seventeenth century, stood in the Watergate until its demolition in 1966.

but, this notwithstanding, it was bought by the Town Council in 1964 and demolished in 1967 along with the neighbouring Bridgend Church. The site of church and house is now occupied by the flats of Bridgend Court and the high-density housing behind it.

Nearby, but south of the bridge and occupying an elevated site above what is now Gowrie Street, was the mansion house of Potterhill whose name can still be seen on the lintel of the gate by the main road. The house would appear to have been built in the mid eighteenth century by a Mr Mercer, a sheriff-substitute for Perth, and, by the early nineteenth, was being rented by family

Brahan House was built for a member of the Pullar family in 1898 on elevated ground on what was then open country beside the road to Crieff. The grounds were later developed by Perth Technical College.

members of the chief of Clan Donnachaidh. It was acquired by the Town Council in the 1930s and requisitioned shortly after by the War Department. On its return to the Council after the war, it was converted into four flats and finally demolished in 1961 to make way for a multistorey block of flats. Like Bridgend House, it too was a victim of the housing crisis of that period.

By the Dundee Road and virtually opposite the entrance to Fairmount Road stood Garry or Glengarry Cottage, the lowland home of Colonel Alexander Ranaldson Macdonnell of Glengarry, the Oxford-educated chief of the Macdonnells of Glengarry on whom Scott modelled a fictional clan chief in his novel *Waverley*. Following his death in 1828, the house was bought by the 4th Duke of Atholl whose attempts to use it as a base for shipping timber from his Highland estates were thwarted by the Town Council. It was later the home of Professor Archibald Sandeman who gave his name to Perth's first free public library.

Across town and enjoying a position high above the Crieff Road was the enormous mansion house of Brahan. Built in 1898 for Rufus Pullar, son of Sir Robert, it was named after the Ross-shire birthplace of his paternal grand-

Marshall Cottage, later known as Rodney Lodge, was one of the finest dwellings on the east bank of the Tay at Perth. It was a large L-shaped house with woods and extensive gardens to the south. One can understand the owner's anger when the Victoria Bridge ploughed through the middle of it.

mother and distinguished by its Arts and Crafts style complete with green roof tiles. The National Health Service took it over in around 1948 for use as a convalescent home and subsequently sold the house and grounds in 1967 to Perth Technical College for their new campus. It was virtually derelict by the time it was demolished in 1970.

Several other large houses – Hamilton House, Viewlands House, Cornhill House, Blackfriars House, Pitcullen House, Springland, Ardchoille, Cleeve, Rio and Bowerswell to name but a few – have either been demolished, converted to alternative uses or subdivided into smaller dwellings in the past century. The redistribution of wealth in the same period and the virtual disappearance from Perth of particularly wealthy manufacturers, merchants and businessmen have made such grand private residences unaffordable to all but a very few.

CHAPTER 5

THE GOVERNANCE
OF PERTH

One of the biggest losses to Perth in recent years has been its diminution in status from a city and royal burgh to a mere town, albeit the largest, within the Perth and Kinross Council area. Perth is believed to have enjoyed the status and privileges of a royal burgh since the 1120s in the time of David I, though the earliest surviving charter – or quite possibly the first charter – confirming those privileges dates from between 1205 and 1210 during the reign of William the Lion. Taking the latter date as the *terminus ante quem*, the town celebrated the 800th anniversary of that charter in 2010.

Royal burghs were abolished in the reorganisation of local government in 1975, as was Perth's city status by default, there being only four officially designated cities in Scotland from that time, not including Perth. Stirling and Inverness have since been added to the exclusive list and, at the time of writing, Perth is awaiting the outcome of an application for the restitution of city-hood. Unlike its royal burgh status which has a charter to back it up, Perth's historical claim to be accepted as a city has been open to question and questioned it certainly has been. Nowadays, those in its favour point to the Golden Charter of 1600 the wording of which could be said to enshrine its city status. However, much depends not just on the translation of the Latin but also on whether those writing in 1600 could conceive of a difference between large town and city.

The charter of 1600 notwithstanding, the magistrates of Perth had no objection to Perth being called a town until very approximately the turn of the nineteenth century. The evidence is there in several written sources, including two old maps of Perth – one dated 1792 which is of the 'ancient town of Perth' and the other, of 1807, of the 'city of Perth'. True, there is a reference in the Council minutes of 1773 to the formation of a city guard but this was an isolated use of the term until the early 1790s when a distinct change can be detected. In

The fourteenth-century copy of the charter of c. 1210, granted by William the Lion, which confirms Perth's status as a royal burgh. Courtesy of Perth and Kinross Council Archive

1791, for example, the magistrates decide to award themselves gold chains with the town's crest on them, with a double chain for the provost, in order to be like other large towns in Scotland. The most telling piece of evidence, though, is a Council minute of 1792 which refers to the 'Council of the City of Perth', the word 'town' having been scored out. One of the first recorded challenges to the claim to city status was received by the Council in 1809. It was appended to a letter from the secretary of William Adam MP who wrote, 'I think it would also be better for you to let him [presumably Adam] have the grounds on which you mean to have Perth called a city.' Adam was not only the Member of Parliament for Kincardineshire but also the Lord Lieutenant of Kinross-shire and it may well have been this latter office which caused him to query the claim of a neighbouring town. In reply to Adam's secretary, the provost wrote, 'With regard to the grounds upon which we wish Perth called a city I hope the

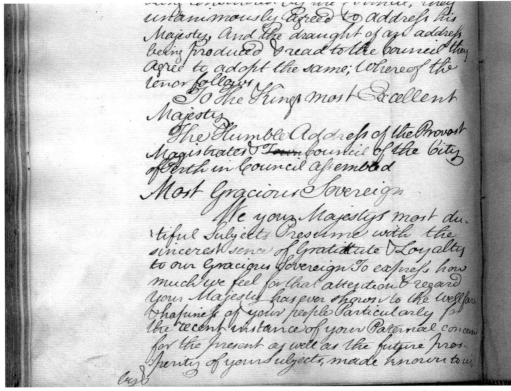

Was this the moment in municipal thinking when Perth became a city? This extract from the Town Council minutes of 1792 shows the wording of an address to the king in which 'town' is scored out and replaced with 'city'. Courtesy of Perth and Kinross Council Archive

enclosed excerpt from one of our royal charters will be sufficient.'

As one of the earliest of royal burghs and as one of the former chief towns of the kingdom, Perth enjoyed a status second only to Edinburgh in the Convention of Royal Burghs. The larger towns regularly had to be reminded of this, such as Glasgow in the 1790s which disputed Perth's right to occupy the seat next to Edinburgh in the Convention. Finally, in 1801, Provost Thomas Hay Marshall, Perth's commissioner to the Convention, insisted on taking his rightful place next to the commissioner for Edinburgh, brandishing a document from James VI to prove his claim and insisting that it be recorded in the Convention's minutes. A further reminder about Perth's status within the Convention was made in 1822 when the town clerk of Perth wrote to the lord provost of Edinburgh to say he trusted there would be 'no deviation from the traditional practice'. No reply is recorded but the minutes state that nothing 'derogatory to the rank or place of this burgh' had been attempted.

Another indication of Perth's new conceit of itself was the adoption of the title of lord provost for the chief magistrate which seems to have occurred in around 1802. There had been the occasional earlier references but, from this time onwards, it was used with increasing regularity by the magistrates themselves. The issue came to a head in 1836 when the Court of Session debated whether Perth had any right to a lord provost and, thanks to the arguments of sheriff clerk, James Patton, the law lords accepted the status quo with only two dissenting. The argument was based on Perth's historic rank within the medieval kingdom, on long usage, on the fact that the title was accepted by the king when the lord provost was presented to him in Edinburgh in 1822 and primarily because of the use of the term in the legal documentation concerning the establishment of the Royal Lunatic Asylum in Perth which seemingly passed unqueried through the great departments of state.

The Town Council governed Perth from its earliest days as a royal burgh until its final dissolution in 1975. By way of a thumbnail sketch, the Council originally consisted of members of the merchant Guildry, out of whose number magistrates, bailies and a provost were elected. In time, the trades of the town were represented on the Council, drawn from seven of the eight Incorporated Trades. The eight Incorporations comprised: the hammermen – mainly metal workers, jewellers and watchmakers; the bakers; the shoemakers; the fleshers; the glovers – which included skinners; the wrights – consisting mainly of those employed in building trades, such as masons, joiners, glaziers, slaters and plasterers, but also, oddly, barbers; the tailors; and the weavers. Although the Council had its own headquarters at the Council House, its constituent groups each had their own seat of authority. That of the Guildry was the Guild Hall which still stands proudly – if perhaps invisibly today – on the south side of the High Street, a little to the east of King Edward Street. The present building was erected in 1908, replacing an earlier Guild Hall on the same site. The Incorporated Trades had their own halls and meeting places, some of which at least are still in use.

Of the trades, the hammermen, bakers and glovers were regarded as the big three and each enjoyed the right of having a representative on the Council. The wrights, tailors, fleshers and shoemakers were regarded as the small trades and shared a councillor between them. The weavers were excluded from the Council in 1658 simply, it seems, as a means of ensuring that the merchant councillors always had a majority over the trades with 14 of the 26 seats. Any lingering sense of democracy in the Council was further dispelled by the practice known as the 'beautiful order' which was nothing less than a further sidelining of the trades by a small number of merchant councillors. This clique, consisting of at least six of their number, plus the chairman who exercised a casting vote, obliged any opposing merchant councillors to vote with them and thus, as the trades saw only too well, a mere seven men could effectively control all the major decisions of the Council.

It was little wonder that some who found themselves elected to the Council were reluctant to take up their seats. Others, too, did not wish to accept the additional responsibilities and work attendant on being further elected either provost or bailie and had to be encouraged with the threat of a sizeable fine – the substantial sum of £40 being the penalty for refusal in 1803. The Council minutes of 1804 describe what happened after David Beatson and Duncan Spottiswoode had been elected merchant councillors: 'And a Town Serjeant having been sent for the said David Beatson and Duncan Spottiswoode, Mr Beatson returned for answer that he would come in a little, but after the Council waited for half-an-hour he failed to attend, and the officer reported the said Duncan Spottiswoode could not be found . . . Then the whole Council by unanimous vote elected and made choice of the said David Beatson, merchant councillor, to be Town Treasurer for the said ensuing year . . . and a Town Serjeant having been sent for the said David Beatson reported for answer . . . that he was particularly engaged and would not attend.' Whereupon Messrs Beatson and Spottiswoode were threatened with a fine and told the date of the next meeting. One can almost sense the glee with which the Council elected a reluctant councillor to an even more elevated and particularly onerous position in his absence. Beatson duly turned up, accepted office and swore, as many others on both sides of the Council did at that time, 'that he shall never vote for the continuance of Provost, Dean of Guild, or any of the bailies for a longer space than two years at one time in the same office, and that he shall keep the secrets of the house for the good of the town.'

In the early nineteenth century, relations between the Council as a whole and its constituent parts were a turbulent combination of disputed elections and constant power struggles, particularly between the Council and the Guildry. This was typified in the dispute over the right to appoint the Dean of Guild, one of the most important positions on the Council. The practice had been for the Guildry to submit a list of possible names from which the Council would make their choice. In 1815, the Guildry objected to this and, in promising to 'reform this burgh', insisted that they would vote for their own Dean of Guild and require the Council to accept their decision. And, not only this, they started agitating the Incorporated Trades to do the same with their trades bailies and councillors who had hitherto been similarly selected by the Council from a submitted short leet. The Council, having taken legal advice which came down in favour of the status quo, then obtained an interdict against the Guildry's illegal action. When the Guildry announced they would ignore the ban, the town clerk, Robert Peddie, was sent along to their meeting to make due protest. He tried to read the interdict to them but was drowned out by shouting, clapping and the stamping of feet and, when he asked that his actions be recorded in the Guildry minutes, he was told that 'nothing of the kind' would be done.

Further power disputes arose in 1817 and subsequent years between the Council, the Guildry and the Incorporated Trades, but it was all coming to a head and very visibly so when a parliamentary select committee, charged with investigating the running of Scottish royal burghs, wrote to both the Council and the Guildry in 1819 asking detailed questions about the administration and financial affairs of the burgh and the method of electing the Council. Disputes and petty revolts rumbled on throughout the 1820s, all of which can perhaps be considered as little aftershocks of the French Revolution which shook the fabric of European society, even as far as Perth, to its foundations. Despite standing up for ancient rights and authority, the Council themselves were not totally opposed to change, as is evidenced by their petition to parliament of 1831 to end the system of self-election in local government that is 'now so much complained of'.

Finally, the Royal Burghs (Scotland) Act of 1833 did for local government what the Reform Act of the previous year had done for parliament – the franchise was significantly widened and ancient powers, traditions and customs swept away, perhaps to the surprise of the Council who had not antic-ipated how radically different the new electorate would be. The Guildry and Incorporated Trades continued to exist and look after their members (as indeed to a certain extent they still do today) but no longer had any corporate say in the affairs of local government. Henceforth, the town was divided into wards and councillorship and electoral rights were opened up to a much wider franchise. Governments continued to grapple with local government reform throughout the nineteenth and twentieth centuries, further extending the franchise and adding new powers and removing others. It was, however, the root-and-branch reform of local government, much discussed from the 1960s, which led to the demise of the ancient Perth Town Council in 1975.

The first duty of the old Town Council was to be loyal, principally to the monarchy from where their powers and privileges originally stemmed. Each councillor had to swear an oath of allegiance to the king or queen before he could take office, an act known as qualifying. Loyalty was emphasised through

The lord provost and magistrates of the Town Council of Perth, around 1950, accoutred with robes, ermine, chains of office and highly polished shoes. They include Lord Provost John Ure Primrose (centre front), Lord Dean of Guild David K. Thomson (on his right) and Bailie George Fairlie (front left). They are accompanied by the Town Clerk, Robert Adam, and his deputy, Archie Martin, in dark robes, and by the town officers.

numerous addresses to their royal personages couched in suitably deferential terms and on matters of particular concern to them, usually following the death of a husband or wife, birth of a prince or princess or an outbreak of war or rebellion. They tended to be understandably obsequious in the decades following the Forty-Five when, from a London perspective, the loyalty of a large town on the edge of the Highlands could not necessarily be guaranteed but, by the 1830s, they could go as far as very respectfully expressing a lack of confidence in His Majesty's new government. An address was even sent to the king of the French, following an attempt on his life in 1846.

Next, they had a degree of responsibility for preserving law and order within the royal burgh. Before the establishment of a police force in the early

nineteenth century, the Council relied on groups of inhabitants to patrol the streets at night though, as George Penny recounts, some of them 'got supremely drunk' and probably contributed more to the problem than to the solution. The constables of the town, later known as the High Constables to distinguish them from the paid police force, assisted the magistrates in the keeping of order, particularly during riots, though, as their peace-keeping role gradually diminished, they became more of a ceremonial presence, turning out for major civic events and royal visits. Their attendance each year at the Kirking of the Council is a reminder of the close links with the lord provost and magistrates of old. The batons they carry on such occasions were used in anger in the eighteenth century to quell riots. In 1792, in a little glimpse into crowd control, the Council decided to furnish all 32 constables with shorter batons, the ones previously in use being too unwieldy – presumably when in close combat with rioters. Such measures were not always successful and, on occasions in the 1790s when food was desperately short and riots commonplace, army detachments were brought in to assist.

The Perth police force we know today was set up as a result of the Paving, Lighting and Cleansing Act of 1811 and its amendment act of 1819. These acts gave authority to the police to act within the royal burgh but, as Perth had developed significantly beyond its medieval boundaries in the previous half century, the police found they had no authority in the suburbs, the area around the barracks being one example. In some cases, all a suspected miscreant had to do was cross the street to safety. Police powers were thus extended in 1839 to include the whole of the built-up area of Perth. The police office was housed in the old tolbooth and moved round the corner into Tay Street when that building was replaced by the Municipal Buildings in 1879. The county force, Perthshire Constabulary, was based at the foot of South Street from 1874 until 1953 when they bought the former mansion house of Ardchoille in Bridgend. Both county and city forces amalgamated in 1964 and were headquartered there until 1977 when, as part of Tayside Police, they moved into their present premises in Barrack Street. Whoever described the Tay Street police station as 'an affront to a modern progressive police force' must have breathed a sigh of

OPPOSITE. *The High Constables of Perth in attendance at a Remembrance Sunday service at St John's Kirk in around 1970. Courtesy of the* Perthshire Advertiser *and Perth and Kinross Council Archive*

OVERLEAF. *The massed ranks of the Perth City Police, with Perth's double-headed eagle for helmet badges, pose for a photograph in front of what is now St Leonard's-in-the-Fields Church.*

relief when it moved into the Barrack Street building at the same time.

The establishment of a professional police force had an immediate and major effect on crime as a report of 1837 showed. Thirty years earlier, it said, it was not safe to be out alone on the streets of Perth at night 'but now a single person can walk the streets at any hour in perfect safety' and, after 11.00 p.m., the town was as still as a 'country village'. Hyperbole perhaps, and particularly so when one considers the number of pubs in town and the associated levels of drunkenness but it makes a point. At the time of the report, the police's main focus of attention was on the 60 prostitutes of the town 'about half of whom are drunken, disorderly' and on the town's thieves, some of whom had returned from transportation. A few were children and many more were vagrants passing through. The report drew attention to alcohol being a major cause of crime and lamented the fact that there were only three or four temperance societies in the county 'but they do not flourish'. Their time, however, would come later. Lest all this paint too rosy a picture of life in Perth, we should remember that, on occasions, the ready accessibility of alcohol could turn a boisterous crowd into a threatening mob with frightening speed. One such occasion occurred during the queen's birthday celebrations in 1861 when, according to the press, the city was described as being in the hands of a brutal mob for several hours – a mob which 'assaulted every respectably dressed individual, either male or female, on the streets. On the arrival of the omnibuses from the railway station they were surrounded by a howling mob, screaming "Hats! Hats!" and as soon as the passengers alighted squibs were thrown in their faces, their hats knocked off and often lost, and their dress torn.' The police and magistrates were condemned for their inaction but, even nowadays, there are occasions when their successors can do little against an angry and drunken rabble.

A third duty of the Council was the administration of the royal burgh, a story of ever-increasing responsibilities, ever more staff and constant worries about money. Compared with the thousands on the Council payroll today, the staff in the eighteenth century comprised a mere handful, including a town drummer, a bellman, a piper, town serjeants, keepers of bells, clocks and fire engines, a jailer and turnkey, clergymen, teachers, a town clerk and a town chamberlain. In the nineteenth and twentieth centuries, these were augmented considerably by the appointments of shoremasters and harbour masters, watchmen, depute town clerks, keepers of the City Hall, inspectors of works, city architects, medical officers of health, librarians and all the others required to administer an increasingly complex system of local government.

Those Council officials who today prepare newsletters and update the official website seem far removed from their eighteenth century counterparts, the town drummer and bellman, whose job it was to 'cry through the town' or, in other words, attract attention by loud drumming and impart official information with a loud voice. It is quite surprising to find that such medieval methods were still in use as late as 1857 when a new drummer was appointed, at a time when there were three local newspapers circulating in Perth, full of local and national news. Little is heard of the town piper after 1799 when the Council put an end to the practice of the piper and drummer going through the town on Handsel Monday (one of the first Mondays of the new year which, according to various definitions, could fall anywhere between 1 and 18 January), collecting money from the inhabitants in a tradition similar to Boxing Day. His main function was to play through the streets at 5.00 a.m., summer and winter, and again at 7.00 p.m. One of the perks of jobs such as these was the provision of clothing – a scarlet cloak for the piper and greatcoats for others such as the town serjeants who worked outside. The town serjeants, of which there were four in number by 1800, basically acted as strong-armed servants to the Council and magistrates, fetching newly elected and reluctant councillors, cleaning, lighting fires, taking part in civic ceremonies and processions and undertaking various other minor duties.

The top two officials were the town clerk, who headed the administration and would equate to a chief executive today, and the town chamberlain, who ran the town's financial affairs. Civic finances were frequently a nightmare, well illustrating the Micawberish rule of economics whereby an excess of expenditure over income, even by sixpence, resulted in misery. And, by this definition, the chamberlain had every reason to be miserable. Income from customs, fishing rights, harbour dues, leases to tacksmen, rents for church seats and the sale or feuing of land was not always sufficient to meet the demands on the town's coffers from not just the major undertakings, such as paving the streets, laying water pipes, dredging the river and building a new harbour, to name but a few, but also from the build-up of smaller items of incidental expenditure such as, in 1830, catching moles on the Inches, conveying convicts to the hulks prior to transportation, arranging and binding the city records and providing music at a dinner to mark the election of the magistrates. Money, therefore, had to be borrowed. The Perth Banking Company, the first bank established in Perth in 1763, was the principal source but there were times when not even the bank would come to the rescue and the provost, on occasions, was obliged to use his personal funds to get the Council out of a tight corner.

Money was also borrowed from institutions such as the Bridge

Commissioners and from individuals in the form of bonds. Interest rates usually depended on what the banks were charging and were sometimes a little higher than the banks if money was to be locked away for several years and only repaid after several months' notice – not that repayment was always guaranteed, as is evidenced by one such request being described as 'inconvenient at present'. Another source of income came from annuities offered by the Council which were regular lifetime payments in return for a lump sum handed over by the individual concerned. In 1803, for example, the Council offered an Aberdeen man an annuity of £90 per annum in return for a one-off payment of £700. The economics of annuities were tightened up in the early nineteenth century with the drawing-up of tables which gave the whole process a slightly more scientific basis than the medical report and proof of age that had been required earlier.

The Council also looked after the townspeople, taking a paternal role in times of food shortage when the risk of starvation must have been high. In 1740, the Council ordered large quantities of 'grey pease' and oats from London for distribution amongst the inhabitants, borrowing £800 for the purpose. Similar measures were taken in 1757, 1773 and on several occasions in the 1790s when shortages were particularly severe. This was partly due to a few canny businessmen who were buying up grain locally and selling it at high prices elsewhere, thus causing a local shortage and requiring the Council to import large quantities from other parts of the country. So serious was the practice that the magistrates actually proceeded to the harbour in January 1796, prevented two boats already loaded with grain from departing and bought the grain for the people of Perth instead. In 1799 and anticipating a bad harvest, the Council agreed to spend £1,000 on buying grain from abroad and were joined in this venture by the Guildry and Incorporated Trades. And, as with grain, so too with coal – though the fuel shortages were generally caused by severe winters which froze the river and prevented supplies from reaching Perth. The Council agreed in 1792, 1795 and 1796 to buy boatloads of coal from Newcastle for distribution to the poor and, in a generous gesture, the sheriff clerk of Alloa, in the winter of 1793, sent a boatload of coal to Perth and was made a freeman of the burgh for his pains.

One can sense a justifiable pride about Perth in the early nineteenth century, with its city status, lord provost, and senior ranking as a royal burgh, as well as some remarkably fine new architecture springing up in the new suburbs to the north and south. And yet, as we have seen, the ancient authority of the Council, held directly from the king, was being attacked on all sides – by the Guildry and Incorporated Trades, by the government and by the gathering

The Council House was the seat of civic authority in Perth and, as such, occupied a dominant position at the foot of the High Street. The braid stair can be seen on the left and a pend to the river on the right. Courtesy of the AK Bell Library, Local Studies Department, Perth and Kinross Council

forces of nascent democracy nurtured by the fallout from the French Revolution and by authors such as Thomas Paine whose works were circulating in Perth. And technology and modern commercial practices were weighing in too, an apposite example being the proposal of the railway companies to bring in goods by rail directly to the station, thus bypassing the customs chargeable at the town's ports and harbour. An agreement was eventually reached with the railways but, in general, the medieval structures and mindset of the royal burgh were beginning to seem more and more at odds with nineteenth-century thought and technology. The process that eventually swept away the old royal burghs in 1975 was already well underway in the nineteenth century.

Council business was conducted at the Council House which was ordered to be built in 1694 across the foot of the High Street and at right angles to the tolbooth. Prior to this, the Council had met in the Session House which was then at the north side of the East Church of St John's. The new building was a plain but substantial two-storey structure which looked up the High Street and guarded access to the shore by way of two pends which could be closed whenever required. At the north of the house and accessed from the High Street was the braid stair, a wide staircase leading to the council room and courtroom on the upper floor. Above the braid stair was an inscription apparently borrowed from an old prison in Delft, in the Netherlands:

> This house loves peace, hates knaves, crimes punisheth
> Preserves the laws, and good men honoureth.

This inscription has since been moved round the corner into Tay Street, though whether it is the same which once adorned the Council House or a more recent carving the author cannot say. On the ground floor was the weigh house – the checking of weights and measures, from milk and grain to lime and coal also being a Council responsibility. This bore a Biblical inscription from the Book of Proverbs:

> A false balance is abomination to the Lord
> But a just weight is his delight.

The building also provided office accommodation for the town chamberlain, the town clerk being close by in the High Street. When the building was completed in 1696, the Council ordered a large table and carpet for the council room, to be obtained from London if not Edinburgh, three dozen leather chairs and a landscape painting for the chimney breast. This was indeed a room for serious business. Outside on the North Shore, the trees that were planted there were reckoned to symbolise the provost and magistrates.

The Council House was the scene of a violent flare-up following its occupation by the Jacobites in September 1745. While the bulk of the rebel army were continuing their march south they left a small number under Oliphant of Gask to hold possession of the town. On 30 October, by way of celebrating the birthday of George II and thus showing loyalty to the crown, a number of townspeople gained entry to the town kirk and started ringing the bells. Despite orders to desist, they carried on ringing at intervals until midnight. Oliphant, meanwhile, and the few men at his command secured the Council House where around 1,400 small arms and ammunition belonging to the Jacobites were being stored. In the evening, the bellringing mob started lighting bonfires in the streets. Oliphant now decided on firmer action and sent a party to disperse them, opening fire and wounding some, and provoking them to such an extent that the Jacobite party was suddenly overwhelmed and

The demolition of the Council House in 1839 opened up the foot of the High Street. The Council purchased an off-the-shelf statue of Sir Walter Scott to occupy the space, in honour of the city's new literary fame arising from his novel, The Fair Maid of Perth.

lost control of a large part of the town. The mob then sent a message to Oliphant demanding his withdrawal and the surrender of the arms and, when this was refused, they laid siege to the Council House, firing at it from all angles and pinning down those holed up inside. This lasted for three hours during the night and resulted in one dead on each side and several wounded, after which the townspeople seem to have given up and gone home to bed. The following day, the town was reinforced by the Jacobites.

The demolition of the Council House was first suggested in 1835 by William Macdonald Mackenzie, the town's inspector of works, in a report on the proposed Tay Street. As an idea, it quickly gained popular support and the decision to remove it was taken in September 1839. As a result, the council room and burgh courtroom were relocated in the tolbooth, the town chamberlain was accommodated in a tenement adjoining the town clerk's office and the weigh house was moved to the meal market. Demolition must have started immediately after the decision was taken as subsequent meetings of the Council, from October, were held in the magistrates' room 'presently used as the Council Room'.

In the mid 1870s, after almost 40 years in the tolbooth and under mounting pressure to improve the police cells in the same building, the Council decided to replace it with a new range of buildings, sufficiently large to accommodate all functions of the Council, from the town clerk's office to the fire brigade, and sufficiently grand to reflect civic pride in its centuries-old history and high status. Accordingly, the old tolbooth with its medieval tower was demolished in around 1878 and, by November of the following year, the new Municipal Buildings, designed by local architect Andrew Heiton, were open for business. With cleverly incorporated echoes of both the old tower at the south-west corner of the new buildings and the old tolbooth turret at the south-east corner, Heiton successfully combined the old with the new – albeit in a neo-Gothic style. As previously mentioned, the buildings, which stretched from the foot of the High Street round the corner into Tay Street, were gutted by a huge fire on 23 January 1895, having barely lasted 15 years. With them, sadly, went many civic treasures including regimental colours, old maps and paintings. It was restored shortly after, complete with new stained glass for which the old building had been famed. This served as the Council's headquarters until pressure of space in the 1980s necessitated a removal across the street to General Accident's former premises.

Administration and justice went hand in hand and, indeed, the provost of Perth, by virtue of that office, was also sheriff of Perth with, at one time, full power and authority within the royal burgh to pass sentence even in capital cases. It was appropriate, therefore, that the Council House, which also housed the courtroom, should have been erected next to the old tolbooth, which housed the old jail. The tolbooth was built in 1666 and incorporated the ground floor of the adjacent chapel of Our Lady, a scarce survivor of pre-Reformation

OPPOSITE. *The police office at the foot of the High Street in 1878. The posters advertise building ground for sale in North Tay Street.*

OVERLEAF. *The aftermath of the great fire at the Municipal Buildings in January 1895. There was no loss of life though historians still regret the loss of old maps of Perth and other such items.*

days. It served as a jail until 1818 after which it went through a variety of uses, ranging from a temporary bridewell (a prison-cum-workhouse for minor offenders and the work-shy poor which aimed to reform rather than simply punish) to a police office, though one of its main functions from 1839, as mentioned above, was to act as the Council's meeting place. The tolbooth was thus known by a variety of names, such as the auld jail and the Town Hall (one wonders if Perth was the only place to have both a Town Hall and City Hall), until demolition in around 1878.

The jail in the tolbooth was a problem for the Council for much of the eighteenth century on account of its size, security and condition. In 1810, a report was presented to the Perthshire county authorities describing just how bad the accommodation there was. The basement floor of the jail was known as the laigh iron house and was traditionally where condemned criminals were housed prior to execution. This most feared part of the jail consisted of three rooms, 'arched with stone'. Within each, behind an iron grating, was a wooden cage. Inside the cages, which tapered in height from seven feet to only four, were irons attached to the floor for restraining prisoners when necessary. The small, barred windows were eight feet above floor level, there was no heating and the stone walls intensified the cold and damp, particularly in the room facing the river. These conditions were described in the report as 'a gross abuse' while the very existence of the cages proved how insecure the jail was.

On the floor above was the back iron house, a large room which was floored and arched in stone and also occupied by three cages. Again, there was no fire. On the same floor was the low burgher room, with a fireplace, which was principally used by debtors. Female prisoners occupied one large room on the floor above. It had no fireplace and the only light came from a window in the roof, making it dark and airless and difficult for those who were engaged in spinning. The women slept in a cage in the middle of the floor. Two other rooms on this floor were occupied by debtors who enjoyed the luxury of a fire and big windows.

On average the jail contained 12 prisoners, male and female, some of whom were debtors, some awaiting trial and some already convicted. They were given loose straw to lie on which was changed once per month, blankets and rugs no longer being permitted at that time. The only 'furnishings' were a

OPPOSITE. *A view of the old tolbooth taken from near the river, prior to 1878. The roundel on the High Street corner can be made out immediately to the right of the tree. The men at the left probably hide the windows of the former laigh iron house.*

pail for water, which was refilled twice a week, and a tub to be 'used as a necessary', emptied twice a week.

The fabric of the building was in poor condition with walls and roof described as 'decayed'. This resulted in several escapes, as well as attempts to break out through the walls, the use of cages and the shutting-up and barring of windows. The lower rooms in winter were an 'outrage' to humanity and far exceeded 'any ideas of a place intended for punishment'. The report concluded by saying that Perth jail was not the worst in Scotland but certainly among the worst.

There was a realisation that the jail needed to be replaced long before this report of 1810 appeared. Proposals for a new prison and bridewell were first raised in 1789 and, by 1793, both town and county had agreed to share the costs. The Gowrie House was identified as a possible site in 1802 though following its demolition in 1806 the project seems to have been temporarily shelved. The jail was back on track by 1812, with plans being drawn up to link it to the court-rooms in the proposed County Buildings, and it finally opened in 1818.

Serving both city and county, the new prison was a huge improvement on the old and sat conveniently back to back with the county sheriff court. Stretching between Canal Street and South Street and occupying the space now used as the Speygate car park, it consisted of two sections, the north wing for felons with separate areas for men and women and the south wing for debtors and those convicted of minor offences. Debtors had an easier time of it, being allowed to bring in their own bedding and, if they could persuade friends or family to assist, their own food. Debtors, though, as well as creditors had to contribute to the jailer's fees of a few pence per day. Facilities for all prisoners included a day room as well as sleeping accommodation and an exercise yard outside, all enclosed by a high stone wall. Conditions were certainly better than in the old jail, though just how good they were seems to have depended on when one visited. In 1835, the jail was described as dirty and the prisoners idle, though occasionally, for their own amusement and a bit of activity, they would enact what was known as a 'hell scene' which would require all candles in the day room to be extinguished before they started screaming and shouting in the dark and throwing burning coals from the fire all around the room. Yet, in 1841, all prisoners were described as employed, with the men either weaving or teasing oakum and the women making shirts or knitting stockings. The buildings and hammocks were judged to be clean, as, indeed, were the prisoners themselves who were put into a bath on arrival and given clean prison clothing to wear. They were given porridge and beer for breakfast, soup and bread for dinner and were allowed an hour's access to the prison yard each day and the services of a doctor and chaplain, the latter teaching the younger ones to read and write.

Quickly, though, the new jail began to run into problems. There were continuing questions of security such as the attempted break-out in 1833, following which a lavatory ceiling had to be reinforced with six inches of stone, replacing the former wood and lead covering. There was also an accommodation crisis which led to plans being drawn up for an extra storey to both wings, though the problem seems to have been resolved by turning the old jail into a bridewell. For such a substantial building, its time as a jail was short – in 1887, the government decreed that all prisoners from the county and city, even those sentenced for minor crimes by the burgh police court, were henceforth to serve their sentences in the General Prison for Scotland on the Edinburgh Road which had hitherto catered for those convicted of serious offences only. In April of that year, a large crowd watched as the 18 remaining prisoners, with their belongings, were shepherded on to omnibuses and taken to their new abode. After several years of lying empty, it was converted by Miss Henrietta Greenhill Gardyne into a lodging house, known as Gowrie Lodge, which aimed to help the destitute unemployed by providing basic accommodation in refurbished cells (though still with bars across the windows) together with food and a small sum of cash, in return for a little work. Thereafter, the old jail was used for a variety of purposes, ranging from a Home Guard store to an Iona Community youth club. Regular demolition threats finally came to fruition in 1965 when the grim old building was knocked down and the site turned into a car park. The thick stone walls around two sides of the car park are the only remaining traces of its existence.

The first mention of what is now Perth Prison on the Edinburgh Road came in 1802 as part of the complicated four-way negotiations between the Board of Ordnance (similar to the Ministry of Defence today), Sir Thomas Moncreiffe, whose estates bordered the South Inch, the Perthshire county authorities and the Town Council. The result was firstly that the Council paid Sir Thomas for that piece of land adjacent to the South Inch where the prison now stands. That land was then exchanged for the Gowrie House and gardens, owned by the Board, which were being used as an artillery barracks. The acquisition of the Gowrie House, as we have seen, allowed the town and county authorities to erect County Buildings and the new jail. As regards the Edinburgh Road site, the intention had been to build a new barracks but the large number of French prisoners of war in need of secure accommodation forced a change of plan and the prison was built instead.

Work began on what was known as the depot in 1811 and, by the following

Several years after its closure, the Speygate Prison was converted into a charitable lodging house with cells providing basic bedroom accommodation. Courtesy of the AK Bell Library, Local Studies Department, Perth and Kinross Council

year, after significant expenditure, it was ready to receive its first inmates. The several thousand Frenchmen who were housed there for that brief period, between its opening in 1812 and what was assumed to be the final incarceration of Napoleon on Elba in 1814, had a major impact on Perth. Not only were the daily markets at the prison hugely popular with residents and visitors alike but the prison was also responsible for a booming local potato industry as well as, indirectly, a healthier local diet. When the French departed for home that summer, the potato farmers of Perthshire, who had earned a good income from supplying the prison kitchens, found that their market had all but disappeared. Those in Perth who set up and cultivated kitchen gardens specifically for the purpose of supplying the prison with vegetables found themselves in the same situation. The potato farmers, suddenly having to look further afield than the

Edinburgh Road, discovered a ready market in London for their Perthshire Reds, whose high prices, willingly paid, more than covered the cost of freight to the capital. Sales rocketed, however, when London bakers discovered the beneficial effects of adding boiled and mashed potatoes to their bread dough, in a proportion of one part potato to five parts flour. By the 1830s, thousands of tons of potatoes were being shipped out of Perth each year. Local vegetable growers did not have to look so far afield, instead finding a ready market amongst the local populace. Napoleon's European adventure had some surprising consequences.

After 1814, the depot was used as a store for military clothing and as a granary, though it was also considered as an emergency fever hospital and as a national bridewell for Scotland. The latter idea seems to have struck a chord with the newly appointed General Board of Directors of Prisons in Scotland who, in 1839, began converting the depot, with much demolition and rebuilding, into a General Prison for Scotland which was designed to accommodate all prisoners in the country who were serving sentences of more than nine months. Although not finished until 1859, the prison was already partially occupied by 1842.

The Council was doubtless glad not to have responsibility for the General Prison, having had quite enough trouble from the staff of the prisons under their own jurisdiction. The old tolbooth jail and later the Speygate prison were run by a jailer and keeper of the town's prison, who would equate to a prison governor today, and turnkeys who would have acted as prison warders. The jailer in 1751 was dismissed for corruption, another in 1767 for 'bad behaviour' and another in 1816 for repeatedly allowing 'spiritous liquors' into the jail, while the jailer in 1817 was suspended following the escape of several excise offenders. A turnkey was dismissed in 1833 for selling a pistol to one prisoner and offering to sell a knife to another. Other turnkeys were disciplined for selling alcohol to inmates, for bartering goods and being drunk on duty.

The most reviled judicial official was the hangman who was on the Council payroll from the 1730s to around 1827. He was provided with a house and paid a weekly sum to which was added a fee for each execution and whipping, plus a small amount payable on each shipload of coal arriving at the shore. The hangman executed the law (hence executioner) in a number of ways apart from at the gallows. He was required to whip offenders, the procedure for which was to tie them to the back of a cart at the braid stair and beat them at various points of their journey around the town, the usual route being along Watergate, up South Street, along Meal Vennel and back down the High Street. What may have been the last whipping was described in the local press of 1827.

A petty thief had been banished from the city and on his return was sentenced to be whipped. The hangman apparently administered it 'very mercifully' but, even so, attracted 'more attention and indignation' than the culprit himself. He was apparently paid one guinea for 'his disgraceful work'.

The pillory was also the province of the hangman who led offenders there by a rope and attached them to it by means of a metal band around the waist. There they stood for an hour, bareheaded, with a notice around the neck describing the offence. One hangman, so the story goes, had to pillory his own daughter for prostitution, declaring to the crowd that he was 'clean affronted wi her'. The site of the pillory, which was a pillar anchored in a round stone surrounded by steps, is marked in the middle of the road at the foot of the High Street, though seemingly it was originally a little nearer the river before the Council House was built.

As hangman, he was also required to 'give doom' in the courtroom, repeating the death sentence and then placing his hand on the condemned person's head and saying, 'And this I pronounce for doom.' For the greater part of the eighteenth century gallows were permanently erected on the Burgh Muir, the last execution there taking place in around 1776. After this, the site of the gallows moved to the remaining mound of Cromwell's citadel and then to the foot of the High Street, in front of the Council House. At this time, the scaffold was stored in the East Church and only brought out and re-erected on rare occasions when required. The site remained there until, presumably, the demolition of the Council House as, by the 1840s, it had been moved to the south of the Speygate prison. The last public execution in Perth was that of Joseph Bell who was convicted of the murder of a local man near Blairingone in Kinross-shire. He was hanged in May 1866 and his body brought back within the prison confines for burial. Until the opening of that prison, executed criminals had been buried in the south-west corner of Greyfriars. Public executions attracted large crowds of spectators, not only locals but many others who travelled from other parts of Scotland. In an effort to shield children from the awful spectacle, teachers, on occasion, laid on early breakfasts at school, with tea, coffee, rolls and biscuits, which were reported as well-attended. The last person hanged in Perth, in the Edinburgh Road prison in 1948, was a Pole who had been convicted of the murder of a woman in Highland Perthshire.

Such were the brutal facts of town life. The vast mass of townspeople lived, worked and died within the town, some prospering, others not, but, at the extremes, the splendour of a magistrate in a gold chain and crimson robe was always counterbalanced by some poor fellow dangling at the end of a rope. And 'twas ever thus.

CHAPTER 6

THE DEFENCE
OF PERTH

Location is everything when it comes to choosing a house or founding a town. That first huddle of primitive dwellings near the river, the embryonic Perth, grew into one of the most important towns of medieval Scotland primarily because of its situation at the lowest crossing point on the Tay. The shallow fords at Perth and, later, the bridges were a natural focus for those who wished to cross the river, while shipping, which could sail as far as Perth but no further, found a natural terminus there too. Perth was also, in a sense, a frontier town between the different languages and cultures of the Highlands and Lowlands. Gaelic had all but died out in Perth in later medieval times yet it flourished until the nineteenth century only a few miles away in Highland Perthshire. Perth was also a seat of authority – not just by virtue of being a royal burgh but through its close proximity to Scone where Scottish kings, as late as Charles II, formally assumed regal power. Parliaments were held in Perth and Scone and itinerant kings lodged at the house of the Blackfriars.

Geographically, culturally and administratively, Perth was a strategically important town, a prime target for invading armies and worthy, therefore, of defence. The old castle of Perth was one such defensive measure – not to mention a statement of power and authority – and, until its destruction by the flood of 1209, it had served as the royal headquarters when the king and his entourage were in town. Although very little is known about the building, which was probably little more than a timber construction atop an earthen mound, a representation of how it might have looked can be seen beside the flood gates on the North Inch. Most likely built in the twelfth century and gone by the early thirteenth, its time was short but, even so, after 800 years, the faintest of its echoes can still be detected in the layout of the streets today. The modern street plan is basically rectilinear with streets criss-crossing the central area in a north–south and east–west direction. A few, though, did not conform

Floodwater on the North Inch behind Charlotte Street. This sort of problem has, in general, been less acute in recent times, thanks to hydro-electric dams in Highland Perthshire and the flood defences erected in the wake of the 1993 flood.

to this pattern, particularly Curfew Row and Castlegable which, together with Mill Street, formed an almost triangular area immediately to the north of the early town. The clue, of course, is in the name Castlegable for it is in this area – or somewhere very near it – that the castle, one of Perth's oldest buildings of more than domestic significance, once stood. The precise location has still eluded archaeologists though there have been tantalising glimpses in what may have been associated earthworks. The suggestion has been made, though, that the castle stood in this triangular area and that the above streets were established around its base. While the streets survived the 1209 flood, the castle itself did not.

There was also a medieval castle in Kinnoull, a little to the south of the old parish church and facing towards the South Inch. It features on General Roy's *Military Survey* of around 1747 and physical traces of it were supposedly still visible in the late eighteenth century. Virtually nothing is known of its history and even the wall plaque on the Dundee Road – until recently the only visible indication of its existence – has disappeared.

Also built for the purpose of defence were the old town walls of Perth. Originally consisting, probably, of earthworks topped with a wooden palisade, they were considerably strengthened by the occupying forces of Edward I of England in the early fourteenth century during the Wars of Independence. Robert the Bruce, in attempting to win back control of the heavily garrisoned and strongly fortified town, laid siege to Perth in 1313 and, having crossed the lade and scaled the walls under the cover of darkness, eventually succeeded in bringing the town back under Scottish control. The walls, which he subsequently ordered to be razed to the ground, were rebuilt some 25 years later by Edward III who forced local religious houses to pay for their construction.

These substantial walls survived, at least in part, for four centuries and in no small way defined the size of the town for that period. Even as late as 1743, during the time of Jacobite unrest, there are references in the Council minutes to the town walls being repaired. Shortly after Culloden, though, in the early 1760s and at a time when the repressive laws against Highland culture were still on the statute book, the town walls were already being seen as an obstructive barrier rather than a protective defence. Some sections of the wall, such as that north of the High Street Port, were demolished in 1762 and, in 1766, the year the mercat cross was knocked down and sold and the new bridge begun, the decision was taken to remove the town's ancient gateways together with any other section of wall considered necessary by the magistrates. There could have been few more significant signs of the town's new outlook – civil wars were a thing of the past and the future was bright with science, new thinking, exploration and business opportunities. There are no further references in the Council minutes to the pulling down of the old walls so the assumption must be that little survived after the 1760s. One stretch of wall near Canal Street acted as the southern boundary wall for the Gowrie House gardens and, as such, survived until the early nineteenth century. Another, at the east end of Mill Street, stood until at least the middle of that century and there is still a small section in Albert Close, according to a plaque attached to it. As far back as 1849, it was certainly believed to be the old wall and, while it follows the line, the minimal thickness has given rise to doubts about its authenticity. However, repairs and rebuilding may well mean that, even though

OVERLEAF. *Where once there was a gate at the South Street Port forming, probably, an impressive entrance to the old town, there was, in the later nineteenth century, a public convenience, handily situated over the southern branch of the lade.*

the stone and mortar may not be medieval, the structure as a whole could still be regarded as the last surviving section of the ancient defences.

Access to the town was by means of four ports or gateways within the wall. (It should be remembered, of course, that 'gate' in Scots actually means 'street' or 'road', as in Speygate and Watergate, and does not refer to the old gateways.) The North Port, also known as the Castlegable Port, was at the north-east of the town (close to the Fair Maid's House) and channelled travellers from Dunkeld and the north into the Skinnergate. Proceeding anticlockwise, the High Street Port stood at the west end of that street, approximately where St Paul's Church now stands, and was variously known as the Turret Brig Port, taking its name from the bridge over the lade, and the West Port. It catered for travellers to and from Crieff, Stirling and the west. The South Street Port, a name which is still occasionally used even today, was situated at the junction of South Street and Methven Street. It was also known as the Shoegate Port, a designation deriving from the old name for South Street, and as the South-West Port. This port served two routes – one proceeding along the line of today's Leonard Street to Edinburgh via the Kinghorn ferry and the other going via Kinnoull Causeway and then turning south along Earl's Dykes (until blocked by the railway) to Dunfermline and Queensferry. After today's Edinburgh Road was opened in the 1760s, Earl's Dykes served mainly traffic from Glasgow and the south-west. The Speygate Port or South Inch Port was at the junction of Canal Street and Speygate and immediately opposite the entrance to Greyfriars burial ground. A Council minute of 1761 well illustrates the problems arising from these medieval gateways. Following complaints that the Speygate Port was so narrow and so low that funeral parties had difficulty in getting through and that carriages were frequently required to unload before they could pass between the gates, the Council agreed to remove the arch and widen the opening. In addition to the above-mentioned four ports, a fifth entry point, prior to the building of the bridge, served those coming from the east and north-east, from Blairgowrie, Dundee and Aberdeen. They would have arrived at the North Shore by ferry and entered the town at the foot of the High Street by way of the Council House pends.

Gates in town walls were points of weakness when under attack and some of the town's ports had defensive towers beside them. One stood at the High Street Port which gave its name to the Turret Brig, which crossed the lade at that point, hence the Turret Brig Port, and another at the Speygate Port, simply known as the Spey Tower, which was the last of the towers to be demolished, in the early years of the nineteenth century. A third, an oval construction

A print of 1789 showing the Monk's Tower which jutted into the Tay at the south-east corner of the Gowrie House gardens, approximately at the end of today's Canal Street. It once served as a powder magazine for the Gowrie House barracks. Author's collection

known as the Monk's Tower, jutted into the Tay at the south-east corner of the Gowrie House gardens or roughly at the junction of today's Canal Street and Tay Street. Prior to its demolition at the end of the eighteenth century, it served as a powder magazine for the artillery barracks at Gowrie House. Henry Adamson, a local schoolmaster, wrote a sometimes flowery and occasionally McGonagallesque history of Perth in verse which was published as *The Muses Threnodic* in 1638. He describes a view of the town walls and towers as he and his companions sail up the Tay:

> Up by the Willowgate we make our way
> With flowing waters pleasant then was Tay.
> The town appears: the great and strong Spey Tower,
> And Monk's Tower, builded round, a wall of power
> Extending 'twixt the two . . .

The ports, plus the bridge, were also watched over for fiscal reasons as customs were levied there on imports to the town. The tacksman of each port's customs would have paid a substantial sum to the Council for the right to raise and keep the revenue as well as the right to occupy the appropriate customs house. In 1791, for example, John Crockart paid over £108 for the right to collect the bridge customs from the newly built custom house at the south-west corner of the bridge. Such an undertaking, though, was a risk and there are several instances recorded in the Council minutes of tacksmen being unable to recoup their outlay. One complained, in 1800, that the poor state of the roads near the South Street Port was to blame for his loss and the following year, at the same port, the loss was due to a poor crop and the suppression of distilleries. In 1865, the tacksman of the bridge customs protested that his principal source of income had been from cattle crossing the bridge on their way to market but, following an outbreak of rinderpest and a subsequent ban on cattle markets in the burgh, his income had been much reduced.

A common complaint about Perth, mainly made by visitors who expect rather more from 'the ancient capital of Scotland', is the paucity of old buildings. They are right, of course, and the blame for that can be laid firmly on one Oliver Cromwell who, during the turbulent times of the mid seventeenth century, occupied Perth and destroyed many old buildings as a quick and easy means of obtaining building materials for his citadel on the southern edge of the town. This citadel – one of four he built in Scotland, the others being at Leith, Ayr and Inverness – was designed to hold large numbers of troops which, together with the psychological effect of the destruction of so much of the old town, could have left little doubt in the minds of the townspeople that Cromwell was not to be trifled with. The Perth citadel dated from 1652 and was built approximately where the South Inch car park is today, though it extended a little to the west of the Edinburgh Road and a little to the north of Marshall Place. It was constructed from timber from Falkland and, as mentioned, from the rubble of several of Perth's buildings, including the Grammar School, the earlier King James VI Hospital, the walls and grave stones of Greyfriars burial ground, the remains of the old bridge destroyed some 30 years earlier, the mercat cross and 140 houses and their garden walls. Turf was removed from the Inches to build up the ramparts, an act which effectively destroyed the grazing for the town's cattle and which, in itself, led to considerable hardship. He left the town kirk untouched, probably thinking it politic to stay on the right side of the deity and, perhaps surprisingly considering he was on the outside, the town defences. The whole construction, surrounded by a deep moat, formed a square with bastions at each corner and with sides almost 250 metres long. A pier was built nearby on the river to allow the citadel to be supplied by ship.

The removal of the citadel, which one might have expected to have been done quickly given the offence to the town by its erection, was a long drawn-out affair. Charles II, restored to the throne in 1660, presented the citadel to the town as some measure of compensation for all the damage wrought and, shortly after, the Lords of the Privy Council ordered its removal. Much of the stone was sold off or simply removed by builders (such as the gravestone which was found in a house in the Watergate, which is presumed to have come from Greyfriars burial ground via the citadel) and some of the cannon ended up on a privateer's ship. This, however, still left the ramparts and the moat, which, in time, were referred to as the mound (or Oliver's Mount) and the ditch or trench. The pier, known locally as Oliver's Croy, survived well into the eighteenth century and may have been incorporated into the Coal Shore. The first steps to level the earthworks were taken in around 1780 and were not universally popular as the moat had long been used for fishing and, in the winter, for skating. Judging by maps of the period it seems that the eastern part of the mound (to the east of the Edinburgh Road) was removed first, followed, in around 1790, by the western part. The moat was filled in partly with the town's rubbish and then the earth and sand from the mound itself. The last vestiges of the moat were apparently still visible in around 1805 but they are not shown on a detailed map of 1807.

As with the English Edwards and Cromwell, the Jacobites too were aware of the strategic significance of Perth. They took possession of the town in September 1715 and quickly set about building new defences and restoring the old. A contemporary map shows a defensive zigzag line extending all around the town, running from the Balhousie lade (approximately at today's Atholl Street and Rose Terrace junction) at the north to the remains of the citadel at the south. This too was refortified and the moat refilled by means of a newly cut channel leading from the Craigie Burn. One source attributes these defences to a Jacobite general, Richard Hamilton, who apparently quickly lost heart and passed responsibility for their completion to – of all people – a French dancing master. Perth was fortunate to emerge relatively unscathed from the Old Pretender's escapade, avoiding the fate of several towns and villages of Strathearn which were torched by retreating Jacobites in order to deprive government forces of shelter and sustenance.

In the wake of the uprising, the government too considered fortifying the town and, in around 1716, adopting Cromwell's model, drew up plans for a massive citadel to the north-west of the town, on the elevated ground approximately where St Ninian's Cathedral is today. It was, of course, never built but, had it been so, the Jacobite adventure of 1745 might have been somewhat curtailed. Nevertheless, the government still wanted to house troops in Perth and, as a report of 1723 shows, considered using part of the Gowrie House as a barracks. There had, however, been some dispute over the ownership of this property and, as a result, the scheme never advanced beyond the proposal stage.

Thus, with no government troops to deter them (although the Black Watch had been in Perth briefly in 1743, before marching south to England), the Jacobites once again descended on the town and occupied it in September 1745. Again, they refortified the remains of the citadel and were drilled on the North Inch in preparation for the advance on Edinburgh. This uprising was ultimately responsible for turning Perth into a garrison town as the Gowrie House, having been gifted to the Duke of Cumberland after Culloden, was finally turned into the long-discussed barracks while a troop of 5,000 Hessians – smartly turned-out German-speaking soldiers who were popular with the Perth public – spent several years camped out on the North Inch.

The Gowrie House was one of Perth's most famous buildings. It was erected in 1520 by Elizabeth Gray, Countess of Huntly, and later acquired by Patrick, Lord Ruthven of the Gowrie family, hence the name. The constituent buildings formed a courtyard and, together with the extensive gardens, occupied the area between today's Water Vennel on the north, Watergate and Speygate on the west, Canal Street on the south and the river to the east. The principal access to what was regarded as one of Perth's finest attractions was from South Street.

The Gowrie House's notoriety in the seventeenth and eighteenth centuries, which made it a must-see tourist hot spot, stemmed from what was portrayed as the attempted assassination of James VI in 1600. Much has been written about the Gowrie Conspiracy but exactly who was conspiring against whom is still open to debate. Were the Ruthvens really planning to murder the king or were they the victims of a cunning royal plot to remove a powerful family? The upshot, of course, was that James survived and the Ruthvens virtually disappeared from history, their titles proscribed and their property confiscated.

The town was granted ownership of the Gowrie House and, along with the Murrays, later Earls of Mansfield, became one of the main beneficiaries of this bizarre episode in Scottish history. The prestigious dwelling, which was given (briefly) to Charles II as a mark of the town's gladness at the Restoration, was let out to tenants such as Viscount Strathallan in 1701 and Lady Lovat in

A print of 1789 showing the courtyard of the Gowrie House, one of the town's largest and most famous buildings. It was also a popular attraction amongst visitors keen to see where the events of the Gowrie Conspiracy of 1600 were played out. Author's collection

1713 and yet was also used as a linen manufactory in 1716 and later a workhouse. This suggests that the building's condition was gradually deteriorating and when, in 1746, it was offered to the Duke of Cumberland as a post-Culloden thank-you from the grateful townspeople, one cannot help seeing it as a devious way of disposing of a building that was perhaps becoming expensive to maintain. This is pure speculation but it seems that the duke was not overly impressed with his new acquisition, sarcastically asking at the hand-over if the piece of ground known as the Carse of Gowrie went with it. The duke almost immediately sold the property to the Board of Ordnance whereupon it was converted into both an artillery barracks and the Board's Scottish headquarters. It remained as a barracks for around half a century.

The Gowrie House was demolished early in 1806, some time after the conclusion of those complex negotiations, described above, between the

Council, the Board of Ordnance, Sir Thomas Moncreiffe and the county authorities. Historian George Penny was incensed. Writing in *Traditions of Perth* (1836) he declared in strong terms that doubts about the building's safety were merely an excuse to allow its demolition: 'But the plain truth was, the building has stood for centuries, and would have stood for ages to come. The only deficiency that could be found was in the lintel of the main entrance, which was broken at one end, and could have been replaced in four hours' time: beside this, there was neither crack nor flaw about the whole building . . . The whole transaction was one of the most shameful ever done in Perth.' The mood at the time, however, if the words of the author of *Memorabilia of the City of Perth* (1806) can be taken as representative, was rather different: 'Attachment to this interesting old house is natural, but antiquarian predilections ought not to be for a moment indulged, when opposed by the higher considerations of public utility. Indeed, so much has this mansion been altered and dilapidated, that the identity of Gowrie-house is almost destroyed.' Following demolition, the rubble was used to repair the shores while the site itself, which lay empty for at least ten years owing to prolonged wrangling over costs and plans for the new jail and County Buildings, was temporarily turned into gardens. Whatever the feelings of the antiquaries of the time – and they were surely right to mourn the loss of such a historic building – the sheriff court which now stands on the site is no less an ornament to the town.

One of the first Perth buildings to be specifically designed for the military in post-Cromwellian times was the riding school erected in Canal Street in 1793 for the 4th (Queen's Own) Regiment of Dragoons. It almost immediately became redundant, though, as, around that time, the government announced plans to build a large new barracks for the dragoons and, for this purpose, quickly agreed with the Council a permanent feu of part of the lands of Drumhar at the north-west of the town, beside the lade. The Council were equally happy, hopeful that the new building would reduce the need for billeting. It was opened in 1794 and initially served as a cavalry barracks, complete with accommodation for 200 men, stables and a brand-new riding school. The dragoons were the first regiment in residence and gave their name to the new building – the Queen's Barracks. The queen in question, incidentally, was Charlotte, wife of George III, whose family name is commemorated in the settlement of Strelitz, a few miles north of Perth.

The barracks underwent a number of alterations in its 170-year history, including alternating between roles as a cavalry and an infantry barracks and sometimes acting as both together. Without the horses and associated stabling, hay stores and riding school, the premises could accommodate around 1,000 infantry. The barracks were rectangular in shape, with a central parade ground dominated at the north-west end by the officers' barracks and, lest anyone forget whom they were fighting for, a large carving of the royal coat of arms on the pediment. The entrance was at the top of Atholl Street at the junction with the Dunkeld Road.

The regiment most closely associated with the Queen's Barracks was the Black Watch whose depot was first stationed there in 1830. Under the major army reforms of the 1870s and 1880s, the regiment became officially The Black Watch (The Royal Highlanders), the barracks became their permanent home or depot and Perthshire, Angus and Fife the regimental recruiting area. Notwithstanding their more northerly roots, the Black Watch became established in Perth consciousness as the local regiment.

The Black Watch and the Queen's Barracks were both lost to Perth in the 1960s, mainly as a result of the deteriorating condition of the buildings and the government's inability or reluctance either to refurbish them or build afresh. The problem first became acute in the mid 1930s and was about to be resolved by the government's purchase of a five-acre parcel of land at Spoutwells, near Scone, to be developed as the regiment's new home, when the advent of war caused the plans to be shelved. The immediate post-war period was one of uncertainty and indecision about the future of the barracks. On one hand, in 1947, the War Department approached the Council for permission to extend into the former Campbell's Dye Works next door and, on the other, in 1948, they were planning to reduce the establishment from 600 men to 60. By the mid 1950s, the Spoutwells plans were resurrected – and, indeed, some houses had already been built there – only to be dashed by the announcement, early in 1961, that the regiment would shortly be moved to a new depot at Stirling Castle and the Queen's Barracks closed. There was apparently much sadness on the last Red Hackle Day on 5 January of that year, a day which, according to tradition, commemorated the award of the Red Hackle following bravery on the field of battle in today's Netherlands in 1795. Among the customs observed, the men awoke to 'gunfire' – not live firing but tea mixed with whisky – served to the men in bed by the senior NCOs.

In April 1961, the Black Watch marched out of the Queen's Barracks for the last time, a historic event watched by thousands of spectators lining the streets. The premises were sold to the Council in 1965 and demolition work began in the autumn of that year, the first stage of one of Perth's biggest redevelopment schemes which included the removal of decaying property in the Old High Street area, the formation of the inner ring road and the construction of the new police station. There is, of course, still a Queen's

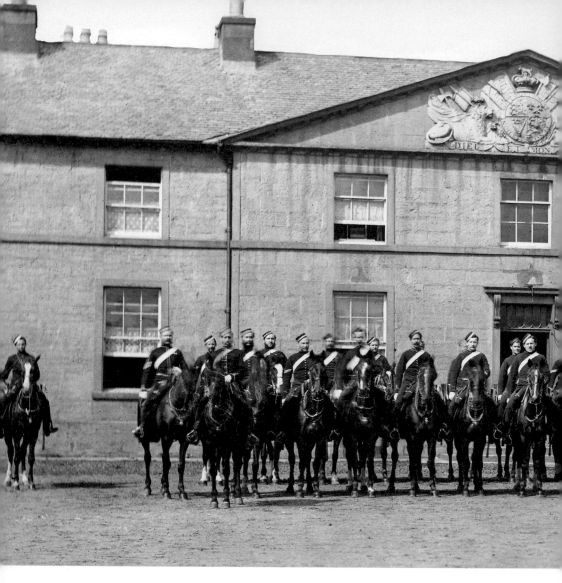

A cavalry unit poses for the photographer in the Queen's Barracks, beneath the royal coat of arms. Spot the odd horse out!

Barracks in Perth though it serves as a base for the local territorials. It is situated on the Dunkeld Road and was opened by the Queen Mother in 1975.

It is difficult to comprehend today, in the absence of army uniforms on the streets and regimental exercises and parades on the North Inch, just how much Perth was dominated by the military. This was particularly so during the main wars of the twentieth century when Perth's situation as a nodal point on the railway network, combined with its role as a regimental headquarters, ensured the constant flow of soldiers in and out of Perth. Many buildings were requisitioned by the army and many inhabitants, young and old, male and female,

did their bit for the war effort. One greatly appreciated facility was the Wauchope and Black Watch Memorial Home in Scott Street which was established in 1903 for the benefit of soldiers in transit. The initial idea had been to provide home comforts in order to discourage soldiers from frequenting the local pubs and prostitutes of the city though, in the hard days of World War I, these were possibly not the first thoughts of battle-weary, bloodied men returning from the front. The building, now flatted, is situated at the corner of

OVERLEAF. *Signs of the military presence in Perth were never far away. These cannon at the foot of the High Street were a relic from the Crimean War. The government sent pairs of cannon to a number of important cities within the Empire, amongst which Perth was apparently numbered.*

the Scott Street car park and its old name, though faint, can still be made out on the side wall.

Military affairs had been much in mind during the Napoleonic Wars of the late eighteenth and early nineteenth centuries when, as in the summer of 1940, there was a genuine fear of invasion from France. To supplement the regular forces, many voluntary detachments were raised, both in the country areas and in Perth itself. In 1794, Provost James Ramsay and a committee of local citizens offered to raise three companies of 38 men each for the defence of Perth and neighbourhood and, within months, had almost double that number. James Sharp of Kincarrathie was appointed major-commandant and his officers included a number of well-known names, such as Thomas Hay Marshall and sheriff clerk, James Patton. How effective they might have been on the field of battle is open to question as the corps was described by George Penny as 'more distinguished for rotundity than speed of foot'. This group of portly gentlemen, embodied as the Royal Perth Volunteers (not to be confused with the Perthshire Volunteers which, as the 90th Regiment of Foot, saw much active service overseas and is commemorated in the monument on the North Inch, erected to mark the centenary of its formation), based themselves in the old Canal Street riding school which had recently been vacated by the dragoons. The site of this building has been occupied in more recent times by Love's Auction Rooms. The Council were proud of their volunteers and, in 1795, agreed to provide the regimental colours, complete with the Perth coat of arms on them. They followed this up in 1803 by voting the considerable sum of £150 for the purpose of buying the regiment greatcoats and knapsacks. The Volunteers reciprocated by helping the magistrates to quell riots among the citizenry and later, in 1811, they presented their old clock to the Council who displayed it in the Seminaries at Rose Terrace.

When concerns about invasion were reawakened in 1802, a second battalion of volunteers was raised, consisting mainly of local tradesmen under the command initially of Provost Fechney and later of Thomas Hay Marshall. Another provost, John Caw, raised a company of musketry who, perhaps on account of a reluctance to turn out, were known as Captain Caw's Invisible Riflemen. Captain Young of Bellwood, whose home was a large property on elevated ground on the east bank of the Tay, raised a company of 80 men and officers, complete with four cannon, to form a unit known as the Kinnoull Rock Artillery. The weaponry was later fired from Bellwood on major public celebratory occasions such as Queen Victoria's visit to Perth in 1842 and, four years later, when a House of Commons committee rejected the use of the South Inch for the General Station.

The militia barracks in Victoria Street with the gas works in the background.

The militia was the army's reserve force, somewhat different from the above-mentioned volunteers. Membership could indeed be voluntary but a degree of coercion was required at times of national crisis when reserve troops were necessary, such as in the seventeenth and eighteenth centuries during times of Covenanting and Jacobite unrest. The militia was embodied again in 1802 to help meet the threat of French invasion and on other occasions in the nineteenth century, including in the 1850s at the time of the Crimean War and Indian Mutiny. This led to disquiet in Perth about the requirement to provide billets for the militia and resulted in a petition to parliament from the Council pointing out that billeting was neither good for the town nor for the soldiers themselves who, when not in a barracks, were relatively free from military discipline. It seems that the accommodation problem was resolved by the opening of the militia barracks, in 1856, on the north side of Victoria Street between Scott Street and James Street. These barracks were demolished in 1895 and subsequently replaced with the handsome Co-operative Society housing block known as Unity Place.

Perth was described as 'lively' during the annual training of the militia which generally took place on one or other of the Inches, though not with the blessing of the tacksmen and cowfeeders who frequently complained of damage to the grazings. Many of the men were from Dundee and were described as arriving looking scruffy and down at heel. However, after a few weeks of regular food and training and resplendent in military uniform, the contrast in their appearance was noticeable. They were paid for their service at the end of the training period when, liberated from military discipline and with cash in their pockets, they resorted to the pubs of Perth which reaped the benefit, even if the local residents did not. In time, the military authorities learned to march the Dundonians of the militia to the station and make sure they were on the train home before any cash was handed over.

A petition by local cowfeeders to the Council in 1874 drew attention to the serious damage caused by military exercises – and by those spectating – on large areas of both Inches over a period of several years. The Council imposed restrictions on the military use of the Inches which, in turn, incurred complaints from commanding officers. The following year, the Perthshire Rifle Volunteers asked if the Council would sell them the City Hall for use as a drill hall and, when that proposal was rejected, the Volunteers then received permission to erect a purpose-built drill hall on a vacant piece of land in Tay Street, close to Greyfriars burial ground. This, the first building in the line of what was to be called South Tay Street, was built 'in the Italian style' with three bays to the front, each with a large window. As a large hall, it also served on occasions as a venue for public meetings, such as in 1893 when Lord Randolph Churchill deployed his oratorical skills so powerfully against the case for Irish Home Rule. By the early twentieth century, the drill hall had evolved into premises for the Territorial Army and, by the mid 1990s, had been replaced by a modern block which today houses the Procurator Fiscal's office. It could be argued that the completion of this most recent building, which, unlike the earlier ones on that site, broadly conforms in style and size to the rest of Tay Street south of County Buildings, marks the completion of the street as a whole – as it may possibly have been conceived 200 years earlier in the later eighteenth century.

When the Black Watch vacated the Queen's Barracks in 1961, they all but severed the long connection between Perth and the military which had endured for more than two centuries. The regimental headquarters and museum of the Black Watch are still at Balhousie Castle but military parades, such as the one in 1995 to mark the 50th anniversary of Victory in Europe Day, are few and far between. But, while the army remained in Perth, it could lay on spectacular parades either through the town or on the Inches, watched by thousands. When Queen Victoria made her first visit to Perth in 1842, her carriage was accompanied by dragoons as she made her way through the town. Soldiers again lined the streets when she returned in 1864 to inaugurate the Albert Memorial by the North Inch and they had been much in evidence the previous year, together with their bands, at royal wedding celebrations on the North Inch. Volunteer reviews were also occasions for the military to show off their uniforms and their prowess in battle. There was a great Scottish volunteer review in Holyrood Park in Edinburgh in 1860 in which 170 Perth volunteers took part and, in 1868, Perth hosted a review of the volunteers of Fife, Perthshire and Angus. On this occasion, around 4,000 soldiers from the three counties marched through the town from the South Inch to the North Inch where they stood for inspection and then staged a mock battle across both sides of the river. They were cheered on by around 20,000 spectators.

In general, the townspeople rubbed along with the military though there were the inevitable moments and periods of friction. Invading forces such as Cromwell's were naturally unpopular, as were Jacobite armies in a town whose instincts were basically pro-government. There is a reference in the Council minutes of 1777 to a dispute between the magistrates and one Major McBean of the artillery who was accused of insulting the provost in the public streets, though whether this was typical of relations between town and soldiery at that time is not clear. Billeting was a detested necessity, from which few families were exempt, and remained an unwelcome imposition on Perth residents until the later nineteenth century. It was a particularly acute problem during the wars with France and, indeed, the Council had to supplement the billet master's salary several times on account of the extra work he was undertaking. Prostitution and drunkenness also attended the military and added to the irritation of the townspeople although some would certainly have benefited financially. Irritated too were the regular users of the Inch, the tacksmen and the cowfeeders, who were all too aware of the loss of income and grazings arising from the military use of the Inches. But there was also the glamour of the uniforms, the interest in new arrivals at the barracks, the spectacle of parades and exercises and, in time, a real pride in and affection for the local regiment, the Black Watch. All this has been lost to Perth.

But, for all the impact that the military had on the town, they have been like any other occupying force – they move in, they stay for a while and they move on, leaving little trace behind them, apart from a host of monuments, memorials and wall plaques in churches and other public places with long lists of the fallen.

CHAPTER 7

THE LOST CHURCHES
OF PERTH

Christianity reached this part of Scotland in Pictish times, thanks to lonely Celtic evangelists who, having traversed the glens and straths of the Tay valley, are immortalised in church dedications and village names throughout the area. Whether or not they established a church in what was to become Perth, as tradition asserts, is unknown and there is as yet no firm evidence for it.

One may ask why St John's, still very much alive, should be included in a book about lost Perth and the answer is that today, thanks to its long history and manifold architectural alterations, it would be virtually unrecognisable to anyone who knew it even as recently as a century ago. It was founded, *pace* the Picts, by David I in around 1126 and has since been truncated, rebuilt, restored and repaired on a great many occasions. Its visitors and worshippers have been a roll call of names from British and Scottish history and it has witnessed scenes of violence and murder as well as bearing peaceful Christian witness to Perth and beyond.

Although we have no images of how the church may have looked in medieval times it was perhaps at its colourful best in the century or so prior to the Reformation when the candlelit interior would have been decorated with wall-paintings and statuary and busy with priests and people making their devotions. The 40 or so altars included those dedicated to the best known saints of the Church, such as the Virgin Mary and saints Peter, James, Stephen and John the Baptist, to whom the church is dedicated. Saints particularly associated with Scotland, such as Ninian, Adamnan, Mungo and Queen Margaret, also had altars dedicated to them. The trades, or at least some of them, had their own particular altars, the Hammermen's being devoted to the patron saint of goldsmiths and metalworkers, St Eligius, and the Glovers' to the patron saint of leatherworkers, St Bartholomew. St Peter looked after the spiritual interests of the fleshers who supported his altar with a levy, known as

Patie's Altarage Penny (a local variation on the medieval custom of Peter's Pence), on all cattle slaughtered in the burgh. The Altar of the Holy Blood was founded in around 1430 and was maintained by the Guildry, partly by way of fines for illegal trading. The founder specified that a mass should be said every day by five perpetual chaplains and that a lamp should be hung over the graves of his parents in front of the altar.

Broadly contemporary with St John's was Scone Abbey, across the river and less than three miles to the north. This early Augustinian priory is reckoned to have been founded by Alexander I between 1114 and 1122 and first colonised by monks from Nostell Priory in Yorkshire. It was elevated from priory to abbey in around 1164, reflecting its status as the home of the coronation stone and the place where Scottish kings were properly inaugurated. The very presence of the stone of Scone at the abbey was perhaps the main reason it was pillaged by the army of Edward I in 1296, though whether the stone he carried in triumph back to London was the real one or merely a copy the monks had allowed to be found is open to debate. The abbey was destroyed in June 1559 by a mob of reformers from Perth and Dundee, following which, in around 1580, the lands were converted into a temporal lordship for the soon-to-be Earl of Gowrie. When his family fell from grace in 1600, the lordship of the Scone estates passed to David Murray of Gospetrie, later Lord Scone, who completed the House of Scone, part of which was incorporated, in the early nineteenth century, into the Scone Palace of today. The precise location of the old abbey, lost for centuries, was finally discovered by Glasgow University archaeologists in 2007 and proven to be much larger than had hitherto been supposed.

The abbey at Scone was the first of a cluster of monastic institutions which developed around medieval Perth. It was joined, over a century later, by the house of the Blackfriars, founded by Alexander II in around 1240 on a site immediately to the north of the town. Its lands were extensive, stretching further north to the lands of Balhousie, west to Drumhar and east to the North Inch, and comprised a complex of church, dwellings, outbuildings, dovecot, gardens, orchards, fields and burying grounds, all of which was augmented by the grant of several more acres in the fourteenth century. For such a large area, the full complement of friars totalled only around 12 or 13, although ancillary staff would have added a few more to that figure.

Thus endowed with land, money, grain and water from the lade, it is not difficult to understand why the friars were seen, in later years, as enjoying the fat of the land. It was favoured by royalty too, with king and court regularly lodging there and the body of Robert III's mother lying somewhere within the walls. Famously, though, following the murder of James I at Blackfriars in 1437, the friary – and indeed Perth itself – quickly and understandably fell out of favour, the principal consequence of which was the development of Edinburgh as the modern capital of Scotland.

In the growing religious tensions of the earlier sixteenth century, the Dominicans at Blackfriars seem to have borne the brunt of local frustration at the apparent wealth of those who had taken vows of poverty. Quite possibly, as the leading one of eight Dominican houses in Scotland, they attracted even more opprobrium. One such flare-up was the appropriation of the Gilten Arbour by the Town Council in 1535 for the purposes of archery practice. The Gilten Arbour – or Herbar, as it was also known – stood adjacent to the Inch, separated from it by the Balhousie lade, and was reckoned to have been the garden of the old castle of Perth. Following the destruction of the castle in 1209, it ended up as part of the lands of Blackfriars and was immortalised in Scott's *The Fair Maid of Perth* as the location from where Robert III viewed the Battle of the Clans in 1396. It was situated approximately at the junction of Atholl Street and Rose Terrace. In the arbitration which followed, the argument of the Dominican friars who claimed ownership since time immemorial was accepted by those sitting in judgment. There were instances, too, of petty provocation, such as when the friars discovered that ground they had tilled and sowed with barley had been surreptitiously seeded with weeds. More serious was the occasion when several townspeople broke into the friary, when the residents were engaged in worship, and, amongst other items, stole a large pot from the fire, complete with meat bubbling away inside, and paraded it through the town. Such a blatant display of hostile derision shows just how unpopular the Dominicans were prior to the Reformation.

Chronologically, the second religious order established in Perth was that of the Carmelites, or Whitefriars, whose friary, according to tradition, was founded in 1262 by Richard, bishop of Dunkeld. He made land available for them at Tullylumb to the north-west of the town, the precise location of which, lost for centuries, was discovered during excavations in 1982 prior to the construction of the Whitefriars industrial estate. At half a mile from the town walls, the Carmelites were the most distant of Perth's four religious houses. According to medieval sources, their buildings were richly decorated and their lands included orchards and gardens, thus providing both spiritual and physical sustenance to those within the walls. The old name for this part of Perth, Dovecotland, suggests that the friars also had a plentiful supply of pigeons. The bishops of Dunkeld, whose principal residence was the rather more austere tower house on the island in the middle of Clunie Loch, made much use of the friary which acted, for a period, as not only their alternative town house in Perth but, during more turbulent times, as the headquarters of the diocese of Dunkeld. Their main town house, however, was in Fountain Close (off South Street) and it survived, if only partially, as a linen stamp office until the early nineteenth century.

After a century and a half, the Carmelites and Dominicans were joined by Scotland's only community of Carthusians whose monastery, reputedly a very fine construct, was built at the south-west of the town, possibly a little to the south of where the King James VI Hospital now stands. The lands around it are reckoned to have encompassed the area, very approximately, between County Place and Canal Crescent to the north, Marshall Place and King's Place to the south, Scott Street to the east and the old Pomarium to the west. The House of the Valley of Virtue – or the Perth Charterhouse, as it came to be known – dates from 1429 though it had first been approved three years earlier by the head of the order, the Prior of the Grande Chartreuse. James I was fully behind the project, having perhaps been inspired by their asceticism whilst in captivity in England, and he not only provided large sums of his own money but encouraged others, rather forcefully it is said, to contribute as well. Following his assassination across town at Blackfriars, he was buried in the Charterhouse, as was Margaret, the daughter of Henry VIII of England and wife of James IV, over a century later. The monastery was well endowed, thanks at least in part to James, and later was given authority over, amongst others, the St Magdalene's hospital and chapel with its lands and fishings, St Leonard's nunnery and its associated lands, the lands of Friarton and several altars in the town kirk.

The fourth and last of Perth's pre-Reformation religious houses was that of the Franciscans or Greyfriars which was founded by Lord Oliphant in 1460 at the south-east of the town. This was the poor relation of the friaries with resources at the start of the Reformation totalling a mere two acres of land. The impression of poverty is reinforced by the varying levels of monetary payments made by the Town Council to the four houses, with the Franciscans receiving only £5 per year (the Carmelites received even less) compared with £26 to the Dominicans and over £33 to the Carthusians.

Greyfriars lasted for just under a century, succumbing to the violence of the Scottish Reformation which was unleashed in 1559. This was not, however, a thunderstorm that appeared out of a clear blue sky but one that had been rumbling and growing for at least the previous quarter century, fuelled by the brazen worldliness of the Church, the gradual infiltration of Lutheran ideas from overseas and the Protestant leanings of both Patrick, 3rd Lord Ruthven (the influential and long-serving provost of Perth) and the magistrates of Perth at that time. That it was all coming to a head is evidenced by the Beggars' Summons of January 1559, a document which was broadcast throughout Scotland threatening the violent take-over of friaries by the genuine poor, unless, by Whitsun, the friars – described as the children of Satan – had already left.

Many churchmen, monks and friars, knew that trouble was coming and a not insignificant number embraced the new religious ideas. Others, more cannily, took steps to transfer ecclesiastical property into lay hands. The bishop of Dunkeld conveyed his Episcopal lands as a long-term loan to his kinsman, Robert Crichton of Eliock, whose son achieved European fame as the polymathic Admirable Crichton, and, similarly, the last prior of the Charterhouse disposed of a considerable portion of the monastic lands under his control to members of his family.

These were prudent actions by members of the old guard as by May 1559 the air in ecclesiastical circles must have been thick with tension. The two events which finally caused the cloudburst and almost immediately gave rise to the destruction of the monasteries were a sermon given by John Knox in St John's on the 11th of that month and the poor aim of a boy throwing stones. To preach against idolatry in a church full of little chapels decorated with religious paintings and statues and in a town where the prevailing mood was one of religious reform was inflammatory indeed. According to Knox, whose own eyewitness account of the events of that time is the only one we have, after he had finished preaching, there was an altercation between a boy and a priest who was preparing to say mass. Rough words were presumably said because the priest raised his hand to the boy who retaliated by aiming a stone at him. The stone missed, broke a religious image instead and, in doing so, incited a spontaneous and ferocious iconoclastic outburst which destroyed many of the religious artefacts in the church. The protest spread to the surrounding monasteries which, after two days of rioting, looting and destruction, were left with only their walls still standing.

It is conventionally assumed that the religious houses were completely destroyed at that time but that may not necessarily have been the case. Certainly the buildings would have been immediately rendered useless but it takes time and resources to remove all traces of a large building and it seems more likely that the rubble and any surviving walls would have been used as a convenient quarry over subsequent years by the town's builders. There is also evidence to suggest that the Carmelite friary was saved from complete destruction at the behest of Patrick, 3rd Lord Ruthven, who was, at that time, both provost of

Perth and a keen reformer and who had family links with the diocese of Dunkeld. Nothing seems to have survived of the Dominicans' house – they were particularly unpopular – nor that of the Franciscans who were poor in the extreme. Tradition has it that the gate to the Charterhouse survived and found an alternative use as the south-east door of St John's until it was destroyed at the end of the eighteenth century during repairs. It was also believed that the stone slab which is built into the wall at the east end of the north aisle once covered the royal graves in the Charterhouse, though there is evidence to suggest it is more likely to have been over one of the Ruthvens of Gowrie.

The Reformation, of course, was far from achieved overnight. At the end of May 1559 and for some considerable time afterwards, there were still puzzled priors presiding over their lands and the shattered remains of their religious houses, wondering what the future held for them. But the income still came in and, indeed, the Charterhouse still operated in a limited way until 1602. The long-term future, though, was settled in a charter of the infant James VI of 1569 (confirmed in 1587), who decreed that all the income from ecclesiastical lands, buildings and endowments within the burgh was to go to the poor of Perth by way of the founding of a hospital, that institution which survives today as the King James VI Hospital. The hospital did not benefit as much as perhaps was intended as sizeable areas of land had been transferred out of ecclesiastical control prior to the Reformation and, in the ensuing chaos afterwards, further appropriations were made.

Although the first hospital probably consisted merely of old buildings refurbished for the accommodation of the poor, the first purpose-built hospital was erected in 1596 close to the bridge, near 'Our Lady's Chapel, at the shore'. This survived until around 1652 when it was demolished by Cromwell who used the rubble for his citadel. Almost a century later, in 1749, work began on the present King James VI Hospital. It was completed the following year and today fronts on to a relatively quiet side road, Hospital Street, though at the time – a good 50 years before County Place and York Place were built – this was the main road from Perth to the south. Originally used as a home and workplace for the poor and elderly, as well as orphaned children, the hospital directors (who were basically the ministers of the town kirk and members of the Kirk Session assisted by an annually elected hospital master) later rented out the accommodation within the hospital and used this income to provide alms to the poor in their own homes. Thus the hospital played host to charity and industrial schools and may well have become Perth's poorhouse in around 1850 had the Board of Supervision in Edinburgh been more amenable to the idea. The hospital was converted into a number of modern flats in 1975, the

FOUNDED BY
KING JAMES THE SIXTH
1587.

rent from which now provides the institution's income. Until the first years of the new millennium, though, the hospital still derived a tiny income as feudal superior of one or two properties in King Street, which were on former Charterhouse land. Although barely sufficient to buy the present hospital master a cup of coffee (not that he would, of course), those few pennies handed over each year were, perhaps, the final consequences of that moment in 1426 when, in his Alpine fastness, the Prior of the Grande Chartreuse authorised the founding of the Perth Charterhouse.

The surviving lands of the old religious houses have since been put to other uses. The burying ground and yards of the Franciscans were taken over by the magistrates in 1580 for use as a town burying ground, the old one adjacent to the town kirk being full almost to overflowing. The appropriately named Greyfriars burial ground, like those of many other towns in the early nineteenth century, suffered at the hands of grave robbers, desperate to earn money by supplying fresh corpses to local apprentice physicians and surgeons. The consequent complaints from townspeople in the 1820s led to the nocturnal illumination of the burying ground by gas and regular patrols by police throughout the hours of darkness, the costs being recouped by a funeral tax. An association of townspeople was also formed for the purpose of watching over Greyfriars, though there were tensions between them and the police, perhaps over the difficulty of establishing, in poor light, just who was guarding and who was robbing. The rules, drawn up in 1829, stated: 'Every member of the association guard shall at all times observe the utmost civility to the officer of police for the night . . . they shall on no account interfere with him in the execution of his duty.' Furthermore, members of the guard were to make themselves known to the police 'and shall not lurk in dark corners or behind gravestones'. When, in 1845, the sexton reported that it was almost impossible to find a burial space in Greyfriars without disturbing coffins of all ages, the Council initiated the process that saw Wellshill taking over as the main town cemetery. Greyfriars, no longer used for burials, is today a peaceful and pleasant place to wander and admire the graves of some of Perth's well-known citizens.

The Charterhouse lands were utilised for the site of the King James VI Hospital and, later, streets such as Pomarium. The lands of the Carmelites, being relatively far from the centre of town, had developed by the later

OPPOSITE. *The King James VI Hospital with its eighteenth-century stonework exposed. Founded in the wake of the Reformation, this venerable institution was made heir to the lands and resources of Perth's medieval religious houses and performed the role of an early social services department.*

eighteenth century into the small village of Dovecotland. By the early nineteenth, it had its own school and, in 1834, the population was given as around 500. Development there was slow, effectively curtailed by the daughters of one of the first residents who, having established a brothel, earned a reputation for the settlement from which it was slow to recover. By 1860, though, and still at a small distance from built-up Perth, the village had expanded to include housing on the south side of Long Causeway and the new streets of Thistle Lane, Rose Lane and Whitefriars Street.

The development of the Dominican lands transformed Perth from a medieval town to a Georgian city but, long before this took place, it was necessary to resolve the dispute between the Council, who seem to have acquired them along with the Charterhouse lands, and the hospital, who wanted them back. In 1730, the Court of Session ordered the Council to cede possession which they reluctantly did, having decided not to take the case to the House of Lords. In 1788, the lands of Blackfriars were sold to Thomas Anderson, the father-in-law of Thomas Hay Marshall, who together proceeded to lay out and build the new Georgian suburb to the west of the North Inch.

Besides the town kirk and the religious houses, there were several medieval chapels in the neighbourhood of Perth which were linked to refuges for travellers and the infirm and, although they have long since disappeared, a few are still remembered in street names in various parts of the city. St Magdalene's was situated south of Perth, originally in open country, though, had it survived, it would today be fairly close to Glenturret Terrace. The nunnery of St Leonard's, lying due west of the South Inch, stood beside the old road to Edinburgh and was founded before 1296. Both, as has been said, came under the wing of the Perth Charterhouse. St Paul's was founded in 1434 at the north-west corner of Newrow. St Catherine's, which lay on the north-west side of Perth approximately on the line of the inner ring road between Dunkeld Road and the Old High Street, dated from around 1535 and was the last chapel to be built in pre-Reformation Perth. Closer to the heart of the old town were the chapels of the Holy Cross, north of the South Street Port, of Loretto (known locally by the curious corruption of Allariet) at the west end of South Street close to where That Bar is situated, of St Lawrence in Castlegable, of St James, to the south of the town kirk, and of St Ann which, lying between the

OPPOSITE. *A pre-1878 view of the tower of the chapel of Our Lady at the foot of the High Street, one of the last medieval religious buildings in Perth, though adapted at that time for Council use. Courtesy of the AK Bell Library, Local Studies Department, Perth and Kinross Council*

vennel of that name and today's St John Street, was also close to the kirk. The footings of Loretto were apparently discovered by a local businessman in the nineteenth century who, true to the principles of the free market, sold the large quantities of human bone he found there for sixpence a cartload – for use as fertiliser. Best known was the chapel of Our Lady at the foot of the High Street (on the north side) which as a foundation predated the flood of 1209. The chapel with its medieval tower survived the Reformation and ended up in the ownership of the Town Council who, until the chapel's demolition in around 1878, put it to use as a Council headquarters and tolbooth.

The chapels and religious houses which blossomed in and around medieval Perth were reduced to a very small number after the Reformation, only to multiply again from the eighteenth century. A growing population was one reason but church divisions and the arrival of considerable numbers of English and Irish workers and of Gaelic-speaking Highlanders, each with their own traditions of worship, also contributed.

The first post-Reformation division was that of the town kirk. In 1598, the west part of the building was partitioned from the rest by the construction of a dividing wall, thus creating two separate congregations known as the East and West Churches. A burgeoning workload was shared by the appointment of a third minister in 1716, though this was jeopardised by the above-mentioned ruling of 1730 that the legal owners of the Blackfriars and Charterhouse lands were, in fact, the trustees of the King James VI Hospital. Suddenly deprived of a useful source of revenue, the Council no longer felt able to support a third minister and it was perhaps convenient that he was dismissed for unorthodoxy in 1740. The position of third minister was reinstated when in 1772 the East Church was further subdivided by another wall, thus bringing into being the East, West and Middle Churches. The three ministers of the one parish shared the pastoral care of the three churches until 1807 when the opening of St Paul's at the top of the High Street prompted the division of one parish into four, after which each minister was solely responsible for his own church and congregation.

There was, at this time, a distinct shortage of space for worshippers in Perth's four established churches, a situation which was felt to be responsible, in part at least, for 'the many evils' in the city. An overflow chapel in Paul Street with 1,000 members had already been built by the 1790s but, with the problem still acute in 1825 – there was still a shortage of accommodation for 4,000 people – the Council approached the Commissioners for Highland Churches and asked for financial help to build a new church in town. The reply was short but not particularly sweet, the Commissioners saying they did not regard Perth as being in the Highlands. The crisis was partially alleviated by the construction of an initially independent chapel of ease in King Street in 1835, which quickly chose to affiliate to the established Church and, having done so, was renamed St Leonard's Church. It was further eased in 1839 when the congregation of the former Auld Licht Burgher Church in Kinnoull Street rejoined the Church of Scotland as the Kinnoull Street Chapel (the congregation of which eventually ended up in St Andrew's Church in Atholl Street).

The first move to demolish the interior walls and restore St John's to one single, open church took place in 1889 but was immediately thwarted by the insistence of Perth Presbytery that two new parish churches should be built and endowed to replace the two that would disappear. The proposal was resurrected at the end of World War I and, this time, received the approval and assent of all parties concerned, including the minister of the West Church who, at the conclusion of the work, was to be shunted out to St Mark's in Feus Road, thus leaving only two ministers in charge at St John's. And with the enthusiastic and financial backing of the townspeople, local businessmen and aristocracy of the county (particularly the fraternal Lords Forteviot and Dewar), the creation of what was to be Perthshire's memorial to the dead of World War I was completed in 1926 under the supervision of architect Sir Robert Lorimer. The interior walls and galleries were removed, thus creating the long-wished-for single place of worship for the first time since the immediate post-Reformation period and, externally, amongst other works, the dormer windows and balustrades around the roofs were removed, creating the less fussy and altogether more impressive building we know today.

After the Reformation and until the eighteenth century, St John's, although subdivided into its constituent churches and, at times, both Episcopalian and Presbyterian in government, was the only church building in Perth. When, in that century, religious dissent began to be more openly tolerated, there grew, like spring flowers, a profusion of churches, chapels and congregations. Perhaps there was something in the water of Perth that precipitated religious rebellion as the above-mentioned third minister of St John's, William Wilson – he who was dismissed for doctrinal reasons in 1740 – was one of the prime movers behind the first serious post-Reformation split in the Church of Scotland. Wilson and a small group of ministers, mainly from the Perth area and led by Ebenezer Erskine, distanced themselves from the established church in 1733, principally over the issue of patronage, and were finally excluded from it altogether in 1740. The Secession Church or the Associated Presbytery, as it was known, took root in Perth when William Wilson and his followers built a church on the south side of the High Street, where Scott Street

This lithograph of around 1850 depicts the town kirk with such a degree of artistic licence that it looks more like an English cathedral. Its exterior embellishments were removed during the restoration of the 1920s. Courtesy of the AK Bell Library, Local Studies Department, Perth and Kinross Council

now is. This first new post-Reformation church in Perth was a simple building with a pleasant garden in front. It survived for over 150 years until it was demolished in 1894, following its compulsory purchase by the Police Commissioners (under the terms of the Perth Improvement Act) to make way for the Scott Street extension which was to link up with Kinnoull Street. The new Wilson Church was built in the newly formed Scott Street, on the edge of the old site, and survived until 1966 when it was replaced with a row of modern shops. By this time, though, the congregation had already rejoined the Church of Scotland, today's St Matthew's being the successor to what was once a popular city centre church.

Trying to make sense of the many splits and reunifications within the Scottish church is akin to untangling a bowl of spaghetti so suffice it to say that

This photograph of the old Wilson Church, built in 1740, was taken around 1880 when it was also known as the South United Presbyterian Church. It was situated on the south side of the High Street but set back from the main frontage of that street.
Courtesy of the AK Bell Library, Local Studies Department, Perth and Kinross Council

the Wilson Church divided again over the issue of a burgess oath, leading to the formation of two congregations, the burgher Wilson Church and the antiburgher North Church, both of which split again into what were known as Auld Lichts and New Lichts. The Auld Lichts of the burgher and antiburgher factions united in around 1820 to form the Original Secession Church which finally rejoined the established church in 1956 as St Luke's. This, the smallest of Perth's Church of Scotland congregations, declined to merge with St Mark's and, instead, opted for dissolution in 1958. Their church in South Street, set back from the road and thus partially hidden, is now a Chinese restaurant.

A further split in the established church led to the formation of the Relief Church in 1761 which, in turn, led to a Relief congregation in Perth and, predictably, another dispute and a second Relief congregation. As church

The old North Church – or, more properly, the North United Presbyterian Church when this photograph was taken – was situated in a pend off the north side of the High Street though it was actually much closer to Mill Street. It broke away from its sister congregation over the road, the Wilson Church, in the eighteenth century. Courtesy of the AK Bell Library, Local Studies Department, Perth and Kinross Council

historian Robert Small wrote, in a statement which could have a wider application, 'The whole history of the Relief Church, Canal Street, Perth, [i.e. the second congregation] is a comment on the malign results of divisions in churches, when frivolous grounds alone are involved.' The first Relief congregation evolved into the East United Presbyterian Church which had a very handsome building behind the South Street frontage. The site today is occupied by the southern part of the St John's Centre.

Towards the century's end, the *Old Statistical Account* lists nine dissenting congregations in Perth, ranging from Episcopalians, Cameronians and Anabaptists – whose principles were 'not very well known' – to Antiburgher Seceders, Sandemanians and 'a small society of Balchristy people, who are a species of Independants' [sic]. Around fifty years later, according to George Penny's statistical analysis of Perth in 1841, the number of congregations had further increased to include the East, West and Middle churches of St John's, St Paul's, St Leonard's, St Stephen's, the Kinnoull Street chapel, the Episcopal chapel, the North Secession Church, the South Secession Church, the Original Seceders, the first and second Relief congregations, the Mill Street Independent Church, Methodists, General Baptists and Baptists, First

The Free Middle Church on the corner of Carpenter Street and Blackfriars Street. The congregation moved from this church to their new one in Tay Street in 1887. The old building, much altered, is now occupied by a council department. Courtesy of the AK Bell Library, Local Studies Department, Perth and Kinross Council

Glasites, Second Glasites, Evangelists and Roman Catholics. And there were even more following the Disruption of 1843, that great schism in the Church of Scotland which resulted in the establishment of the Free Church.

When the old divisions were partially healed in 1900 and 1929, the Church of Scotland found itself with a surplus of old church buildings, a number of which have since been demolished. Others disappeared before reunion when those basic and often hastily built churches were replaced with something more substantial and certainly more prestigious. One such was the Free West Church in Mill Street, opposite Guard Vennel, which was not only underway within days of the actual split but open by October 1843. With accommodation enough to hold over 1,000 people, there were so few of the original congregation remaining that the Council briefly considered closing the established West Church of St John's altogether. The Free West Church congregation remained in Mill Street until 1871 when they moved to a new building in Tay Street, now known as St Matthew's. The old building was swallowed up by the relentless eastwards advance of Pullars along Mill Street.

The Free Middle Church was built in Blackfriars Street in 1843 and, like the Free West, moved to Tay Street, beside today's Royal George Hotel, in

ABOVE. *This was the Marshall Place studio of Perth's pre-eminent photographer of the nineteenth century, Magnus Jackson, whose photographs are carefully looked after in Perth Museum and Art Gallery. The majority of photographs in this book have been taken from that collection. The studio was demolished prior to the construction in 1885 of the second Free St Leonard's Church, now St Leonard's-in-the-Fields.*
Courtesy of the AK Bell Library, Local Studies Department, Perth and Kinross Council

OPPOSITE. *Free St Stephen's Gaelic Church in Paradise Place. The congregation had left the Gaelic Chapel in Canal Street at the Disruption and built a new church in Newrow, before moving to this location in 1878.*

1887. This church, like its predecessor, has been converted to an alternative use. Free St Leonard's was likewise opened in 1843 on a site in Victoria Street opposite the gas works. The congregation moved to what is now St Leonard's-in-the-Fields in Marshall Place in 1885.

Free St Stephen's Gaelic Church, so named in 1836, stemmed from the old Gaelic chapel which opened in 1788 in Canal Street (the building is now a nightclub) to cater for the influx of Highlanders dispossessed of their lands by clearances and agricultural improvements. By far the greater proportion of its members at the time of the Disruption chose to follow their minister out of the established church and, eventually, into a new church in Newrow. They built another new church in Paradise Place in 1878 and, in 1886, having ceased to hold services in Gaelic altogether, finally dropped Gaelic from their name. The

St Stephen's congregation ended up at Muirton as part of an outreach programme to Perth's new suburbs, leaving an empty building which was demolished as part of the Pomarium slum clearance in 1958.

Free St Paul's took over the old St Stephen's Church in Newrow and built a new church on the same site in 1900. That building is now occupied by the Perth and Kinross Society for the Blind. As the established church of St Paul's was still going strong at the top of the High Street, Free St Paul's could not, on returning to the Church of Scotland in 1929, simply drop Free from its name. Instead it became St Columba's and eventually united with St Leonard's in 1944. Similarly, Free St Leonard's became St Leonard's-in-the-Fields.

The Knox Free Church began in 1855 as a mission hall in Meal Vennel, supported by the other Free churches of Perth. A substantial church building was opened two years later on a site in South Street, immediately to the west of today's branch of the Royal Bank of Scotland, and was notable for having as its second minister one John Buchan, father of the future Lord Tweedsmuir, the novelist and Governor General of Canada. The Knox Church was the only surviving Free church in Perth after 1900, the congregation choosing to adhere strictly to their beliefs and to their austere style of worship. Numbers began to dwindle, making a move out of South Street necessary, and the old church was sold in 1954 and demolished shortly after. A new church was erected in Tulloch some years later but so poor was the construction that it had to be rebuilt on the same site in 1989.

Of the non-Presbyterian denominations, the Roman Catholic community perhaps had the toughest time. Very few clung to the old faith in the years after the Reformation and, indeed, in a report to Rome of 1677, Perthshire was described as being completely devoid of Catholics. Their revival in Perthshire has been attributed to the 4th Earl of Perth whose espousal of the cause allowed small Catholic communities to grow around the two main centres of the family estates, at Drummond Castle near Crieff and at Stobhall, a few miles north of Perth. By 1763, there were over 450 Catholics worshipping on the Drummond estates. The relaxation of the harsh penal laws in the late eighteenth and earlier nineteenth centuries, coupled with an increasing number of Irish and Highland Catholics in Perth, allowed the first Roman Catholic church to be built in the town in 700 years. St John's in Melville Street was completed by 1833 and, by 1841, had seating for 500 church members. The church was much enlarged in the mid 1850s.

Episcopalians in Perth fared better than the Catholics, though they still suffered in the eighteenth century from the penal laws arising from the links of the parent church to Jacobitism and locally from a congregational schism in

1740 over a matter of doctrine. Episcopalians were tolerated after the Forty-Five if they were prepared to take an oath of loyalty to a non-Scottish bishop and one of the Perth congregations did so, thus earning for themselves the name of the English Chapel. They enjoyed good relations with the Town Council, helped, no doubt, by a generous loan to the Council from their highly esteemed priest, the Rev. Adam Peebles. For a number of years, this congregation occupied part of the old Parliament House before moving, in around 1800, to a purpose-built chapel in Princes Street which was rebuilt on a larger scale in around 1850. At this time, the congregation had also voted to rejoin the Scottish Episcopal Church and the name English Chapel was dropped in favour of the new name, St John's Episcopal Chapel (later Church). The other congregation, those still adhering to the Scottish Episcopal Church, remained virtually moribund for much of the first half of the nineteenth century until resurrected by the appointment of a Durham clergyman in around 1846. Few, though, would have foreseen that, within five years, that small number of Scottish Episcopalians who then met in a hall in Atholl Street would be worshipping in the small but brand-new St Ninian's Cathedral.

The St Andrews Chapel, together with its school, was built near the station in 1868 to provide a place of worship for the poorer Episcopalians of Perth and there were many of them, particularly labourers who came to work on the construction of the railway and stayed. This chapel, which had been hidden by taller structures and thus long forgotten by the Perth public, was suddenly returned to view in the late twentieth century by the demolition of surrounding buildings, though it too has subsequently been pulled down.

The Glasites were founded by John Glas near Dundee in around 1730 and were particularly strong in the local area, establishing their church at around the same time that the above William Wilson did his. It became known as the Kail Kirk, from the custom of serving up a substantial 'love feast' of broth and meat between the morning and afternoon Sunday services. And, for a church that was proud of its egalitarian, non-hierarchical organisation, it was as successful as any in arguing over doctrine and ultimately splitting. In this instance and with a touch of local humour, the breakaway faction – which consisted of mainly the poorer members – became known as the Bread and Cheese Kirk. They worshipped in different locations in the High Street and are still remembered by way of a plaque on the Kail Kirk's old meeting house in the Old High Street, opposite St Paul's. The Perth congregation finally disbanded in 1928. Its adherents outside Scotland were known as Sandemanians, named after Perth-born Robert Sandeman who married John Glas's daughter and who spread Glasite beliefs to England and the USA.

The Baptists can trace their origins in Perth back to at least the time of Cromwell. After a period worshipping in South Street, they moved, in 1892, to the former Opera House on the corner of Tay Street and Canal Street. And there they remained until their church – and, indeed, that whole corner building – was destroyed by fire in 1984. They opened a new church in Burghmuir in 1990.

Methodism was founded by John Wesley in the 1730s and had already reached Perth by 1768 when he made the first of his six visits to the town. On a later visit, he was proud to be made a freeman of the burgh. A purpose-built meeting house was established in South Street where the second-floor arched windows can still be seen and where, at street level, the name Wesley Place can still be made out over the pend. A new Gothic-style church was opened in 1880, just around the corner in the recently opened new section of Scott Street, though the old meeting house was kept on until 1958.

The Evangelical Union – or the Morisonian Kirk, so named from its founding father – was a peculiarly Scottish church, originating in a dispute in the United Secession Church in Kilmarnock. The Perth church, on the present Perth Theatre site, was built in the Gothic style in around 1862. It merged in the later 1890s with the Congregational Union of Scotland whose church at the foot of Mill Street, after several reincarnations, was demolished to make way for the second (and present) Marks & Spencer store. The merger was marked by the construction of the Congregational Church in Kinnoull Street and the demolition of the Evangelical Union church in the High Street, both in around 1899.

Mention should be made of the established church's Session House, the one ecclesiastical building in Perth that was not a place of worship but, rather, where the administration of the town's churches was carried out and church records kept (sensibly, perhaps, there was, for a time, only one Kirk Session and one church register despite the proliferation of churches). The Session House was originally on the north side of St John's and, prior to demolition, was described by historian Thomas Hay Marshall as 'a dismal-looking adjunct projecting into the street, its windows strongly grated with iron bars'. It was demolished at the time the Kirkgate was widened and subsequently rebuilt on the south side, though so poor was the quality of building that, in around 1844, it too had to be demolished. Its four storeys had accommodated not only the Kirk Session but Academy staff, a public library and meeting rooms for organisations such as the Literary and Antiquarian Society. In its place was built, as part of the City Hall development at the flesh market, a new bow-fronted session house which, though much smaller, presided over the market square –

The Evangelical Union Church in the High Street which was demolished to make way for the present Perth Theatre. Courtesy of the AK Bell Library, Local Studies Department, Perth and Kinross Council

or City Hall Square, as it came to be known – in a rather grander manner than did the City Hall opposite. It survived until the early years of the twentieth century when, together with the old City Hall, it was demolished to make way for the new. The Lesser City Hall now occupies the site, though possibly for not much longer.

As with the military in Perth, it is hard to comprehend nowadays, when there are so few city centre churches and when Sundays are little different in character to weekdays, just how many churches and places of worship there were within the town and the extent of the grip that the Church had on local society, particularly in the later nineteenth century. Not everyone went to church, of course – apart from a few atheists in town, there were a considerable number of rival attractions, even on Sundays, when pubs were open and steamboats and trains operating. Most Perth folk, though, had a healthy respect for their churchmen and a loyalty to them which often extended beyond an attachment to a building. Had the converse been true, we would not have had so many churches and this chapter would not have been so long – or so complicated.

CHAPTER 8

THE LOST SCHOOLS
OF PERTH

Those who attended Tom McCrea's history classes at Perth Academy – he, the medievalist and stalwart of Perthshire Cricket Club affectionately known as Long Tom – might remember him saying that, like the universities of Oxford and Cambridge, the Academy had its beginnings in the twelfth-century Renaissance, a claim which jarred with pupils who, every day, entered the school by way of a door superscribed with the year 1932. The building was, of course, relatively recent and even the school name was only two centuries old but the flame of education had, indeed, been burning in Perth since the twelfth century and it had latterly fallen to the Academy to carry the torch.

The church, in medieval times, catered for both the spiritual needs of the people and its own need of an educated elite of priests and administrators. The duality persists to this day in the words 'clerk' and 'clerical', which can apply equally to a clergyman or an office worker. Church and school thus existed side by side in early times and this was certainly the case in Perth where the earliest mention of a school is in a charter of 1150 which refers to the churches of Perth and Stirling and the schools attached to them. In time, the Town Council became involved in the practical aspects of running and financing what had become known as the Grammar School, leaving the church to supervise the teaching, and this arrangement continued until after the Reformation though presumably with a different perspective. Curiously, early documents refer to grammar schools in the plural though whether there was just one grammar school with two buildings or actually two separate grammar schools we do not know. There was, however, a grammar school building near the corner of Speygate and South Street and another nearby on the corner of South Street and St Ann's Lane. References to the old grammar school site nowadays generally apply to the latter.

By the mid eighteenth century, the Grammar School was teaching a strongly classical curriculum where Latin (taught from the earliest days) and, at times, Greek and Hebrew were some of the principal subjects offered, though, as the purchase of telescopes, globes and maps in the 1750s suggests, there was a modicum of science teaching too. And, while this would have prepared boys well enough for careers in law and the church, it was increasingly at odds with the worlds of science, technology and commerce currently opening up in Scotland in the wake of the Union. The winds of change that made the Glasgow tobacco lords rich and turned Adam Smith's mind to the principles of capitalism were now stirring in Perth and ushered in not just a new school but a new type of school where the sciences would be given equal weighting with the classics.

An Academy for Literature and the Sciences was thus founded in Perth by resolution of the Town Council in 1760. A broad curriculum included the traditional subjects of philosophy, poetry, rhetoric, logic and history, to which was added natural philosophy (this pleasantly antiquated term was still in use in at least one of our older universities in recent years), various branches of mathematics such as 'vulgar and decimal fractions', trigonometry, geometry, algebra, navigation and astronomy. If they so wished, boys could keep up the Latin and Greek they had already learnt by paying extra for an hour's teaching every morning between 8.00 and 9.00. Otherwise, Latin was left to the Grammar School.

By 1762, the Academy was accommodated above the meal market, immediately west of St John's, and was teaching in tandem with the Grammar School close by. The Council minutes record both the progress of education in Perth, of how logarithms, air pumps and microscopes were bought, and the issues of the day, from heating cold schoolrooms and the financial problems of a rector to the hiring and dismissal of staff. One such dismissal may have owed something to the prevailing political situation – in 1797 and at the height of the wars with France, the French teacher, Monsieur De Verland, was sacked because 'very few students at the Academy have at any time attended Mr de Verland for instruction . . . and that none of them have [sic] attended him for these several months past'. He was either boycotted by the pupils out of misplaced patriotism or a particularly poor teacher.

The deteriorating conditions of both schools and the lack of any school playgrounds were two of the reasons behind the move away from cramped schoolrooms in the town centre to new school buildings beside the North Inch. The Council minutes record that the proposal to house both schools under one roof had been under consideration for some time and that Edinburgh architect, Robert Reid, had drawn up plans. Provost Thomas Hay Marshall, owner of the

Blackfriars lands, now offered to give the Council sufficient land in Rose Terrace to allow the Seminaries (as they were to be known) to be built. The land would be given free of charge as long as the Council would contribute £1,000 of the estimated total of £4,000, the bulk of it to come from voluntary subscriptions. Funds were quickly raised thanks to over 200 subscribers stepping forward and the town's new school buildings were opened in September 1807. With the appointment of the remarkable Adam Anderson as rector of the Academy two years later, the future of education in Perth seemed secure.

Something is indeed missing from this view of the Old Academy in Rose Terrace. Architect Robert Reid had always intended to finish the building with a sculpture at the top but it was only in 1886 that the clock and Britannia with her lion were placed in position.

The old Grammar School building was, shortly after, converted into a theatre and remained as such until around 1820 when the Theatre Royal in Atholl Street was opened. The old building was destroyed by fire in 1824, rebuilt by the Council shortly after and leased out as the City Hotel until the

1850s. The Academy building fared little better, eventually being demolished to make way for the new Session House which was erected in around 1844 between the old City Hall and the town kirk.

Under the terms of the great Education Act of 1872, the management of the Seminaries was transferred from the Council to the new Perth School Board. It was around this time too that the division between the two schools was ended, Perth Academy providing the name by which it was now to be known rather than the more ancient Perth Grammar School (which name, however, was to be resurrected in 1971). While the Academy may have lost a sister school, it gained another by the incorporation of Sharp's Institution, which came into being thanks to the terms of the will of John Sharp, a local baker and resident of Barnhill. Opened in South Methven Street in 1860, it focused initially on the education of the lower social classes and, while that may have meant an emphasis on practical subjects, they were supplemented, in time, by a good range of academic disciplines too, from Latin and French to science, music and even physiology. By 1882, such was the quality and range of its teaching that it was beginning to be seen as a rival to the Academy. This growing duplication of subjects covered at both schools and the minimal funds with which to teach them eventually called for a degree of rationalisation and it was, therefore, agreed, in 1910, that the Trust, which had hitherto managed its affairs, would hand the Institution over to the School Board, thus paving the way for a full merger with the Academy in 1915. The Sharp's Institution building is now a nightclub, though the name lived on until recent years (and perhaps it still does) through the strict instructions to Academy pupils, while sitting public exams, to give 'Perth Academy and Sharp's Institution' as the full and proper name of the school.

Despite the addition of large school premises in South Methven Street, the Academy in Rose Terrace, now over a century old, was going through an accommodation crisis. The Council considered alternative sites at Bellwood and Muirton Bank, as well as rebuilding anew in Rose Terrace, but eventually settled upon a site at Viewlands. The senior department of the new Perth Academy thus opened at its present site in 1932, while the juniors had to make do with the Sharp's Institution building until their own junior department was completed at Viewlands in 1942. What is now known as the Old Academy has since been put to a number of uses, including as the County Library headquarters and briefly as the local registry office. The centuries-old practice of charging fees was finally ended at the Academy in 1946, as a consequence of the Education Act of the previous year (one of the final pieces of legislation of the wartime government). A curious consequence of this may have been the merger in 1947 of Perthshire Rugby Club with the Academy FP's rugby club, Perth Academicals. The sports department at the school had depended on a slice of the income from fees to support its activities, the withdrawal of which may have added a certain urgency to the negotiations between the two clubs that were already underway at that time. Fees at the Junior Academy were abolished in 1966.

As well as the Grammar School, the early church in Perth supported the Sang School which was primarily concerned with music in the town kirk. That it survived the rigours of the Reformation is evidenced by one master of the Sang School, John Swinton, who is recorded as being asked to sing his tenor line *sotto voce* to avoid confusing the congregation. He was subsequently dismissed in 1582 – not for singing too loudly but apparently for rather more serious faults.

Several charity schools provided a basic education to the children of the poor in Perth. One such school was founded on a trial basis in 1789 by the SSPCK – or, more properly, the Society in Scotland for Propagating Christian Knowledge – with a financial contribution from the Council. This was most likely a school for Gaelic-speaking children as not only was the SSPCK an organisation noted and sometimes criticised for its anglophone educational work in the Highlands but the schoolmaster's house was provided by the Gaelic Chapel in Canal Street and the first headmaster, Alexander Duff, was appointed specifically to teach the children of poor Highlanders. The school, whatever the language of its scholars, was initially planned to accommodate 60 pupils but was quickly overwhelmed by demand. By 1795, the Council minutes record that there were too many scholars for Duff 'to do them all proper justice in their education' and additional funds were accordingly voted to allow him to take on an assistant. Duff died in 1822 and, when Duncan Campbell, the SSPCK schoolmaster in Kinloch Rannoch, was about to be appointed in his place, the Council withdrew their financial support saying they would rather pay the whole of the schoolmaster's salary, bringing him fully under Council authority. This seems to have been accepted by the SSPCK as, later that year, the magistrates are recorded as drawing up rules for the school. Duncan Duff was appointed schoolmaster later in 1822.

By 1825, the Perth Free School, as it was now known, was based in a schoolroom in the King James VI Hospital which, at this time and certainly in accordance with its *raison d'être*, was probably contributing to the school's costs. Reading, writing, arithmetic and English (another indicator, perhaps, of a Gaelic-speaking intake) were taught between the hours of 10.00–1.00 and 2.00–4.00, with classes for older pupils, perhaps those already working, provided in the evening. Thirty pupils were educated free of charge, 50 paid one shilling per quarter and the remainder, as many as the room could accommodate, one shilling and sixpence per quarter – less than a third of the Grammar School fees half a century earlier. One halfpenny was added as a contribution towards coal, while books, pens, paper and slates had to be provided by parents or friends.

Duncan Duff appears regularly in the Council minutes, sometimes complaining about the pupils – as he did in 1831 when he felt too many were absenting themselves in the summer to undertake agricultural duties – and, more often, bemoaning his own paltry salary. He finally resigned in 1869 after almost half a century of service.

There were two other charity schools of note – the earlier foundation being the Stewart Free Trades School which was financed by a legacy from the estate of William Stewart, a Perth man who had made his money in London. The school was founded in 1813 with the specific purpose of teaching children of the freemen of the Incorporated Trades, each trade having an allocation of ten places. The school was situated in Mill Street in what today would be the middle of Kinnoull Street, between the former Sandeman Library and Matthew Gloag's old premises. In 1830, it was described in the Council minutes as 'a charitable institution of great advantage to the city, and conducted by an able and successful teacher'. A later and similarly successful teacher was Robert Shand who went on to become headmaster of Southern District School; such was the mark he made that the latter school, for many years after his death in 1895, was simply known as Shand's. The Guildry too supported a school primarily, though not exclusively, for the children of its members.

The Infant School in King Street was the other main charity school devoted to the elementary education of the children of the working classes. Fees were as low as one penny per week with the poorest paying nothing. Within little more than 20 years of its foundation in 1827, almost 5,000 children, predominantly girls, had passed through its doors and, according to school inspectors, had received an education 'very seldom surpassed, or even equalled'. The school was sandwiched between the King James VI Hospital and St Leonard's Church, on a site now occupied by a garage. The pupils of this school, as well as those of the Stewart Free Trades School, were transferred by the School Board to Caledonian Road School when it opened in 1892.

Despite the best efforts of the charitable foundations, the growing population of Perth in the early nineteenth century was giving rise to serious accommodation problems, not only in the town's churches, as we have seen,

The former West Church school in Nelson Street, which was later renamed Southern District School by the Perth School Board. This photograph was taken in 1993, prior to demolition. Courtesy of the AK Bell Library, Local Studies Department, Perth and Kinross Council

but in its schools too. This was brought to light in a report of the Council's education committee in 1835 which revealed that, of the 3800 children in the four parishes of Perth, over 1500 did not attend school, the problem being particularly acute in the Pomarium and Leonard Street areas. The committee lamented this 'melancholy view of the state of education in this city' which resulted in 'so many hundreds of children being without the means of that knowledge necessary for the proper regulation of their conduct in this world – or preparing them for another'. Council members were quite shocked by the report, some laying the blame for the educational neglect of the lower and middle classes on the disproportionate sums spent on the relatively few pupils at the Seminaries. Following a public meeting, however, they resolved to try to remedy the situation by raising sufficient funds from various sources to build four new schools. This was overambitious but, even so, in 1837, two National Schools were opened in Watergate and Newrow, so named in recognition of the 50 per cent grant received from the government to help fund them. Their stated aim was to provide affordable education for children of the operatives, or working class, through 'the most approved modes of teaching'. Adopting the ideas of 'Mr Wood of Edinburgh', whose methods were already being used in the capital, the schools operated a monitorial style of teaching – tables were placed against the walls, with the teacher's desk in the middle, and 'striking and useful' images were displayed on the walls to impress the youthful mind. Teachers had to be Protestants, their primary duty being 'the development and cultivation of the religious, intellectual and moral faculties of the scholars'. It was recognised, though, that children should not be kept indoors all day and playgrounds were also provided. Three years after his school had opened, the teacher at Newrow wrote to the Council with a number of suggested improvements, including the stabilisation of the seats in order to improve the children's writing and the provision of a 'swinging pole' for the playground.

As with other schools, the National Schools suffered from their own success. In 1851, a church minister visited the Newrow School and subsequently wrote to the Council, saying he was 'truly overwhelmed to witness such a multitude of nice little children huddled into such a small place'. He perhaps over-egged it a little by suggesting that the unhealthy atmosphere would cause 'disease, imbecility and premature death' but was certainly anxious that the Council should either enlarge the school or, more drastically, dismiss one third of the children. The National Schools were transferred to the School Board in 1874, the Watergate School closing in around 1884 when its suburban successor, Western District School (later Craigie Primary), opened. The Newrow School enjoyed a new lease of life as the church hall for Free St Paul's.

Churches also rallied to the cause of education in Perth in the 1830s, setting up their own schools and providing an elementary education focused on reading, writing and arithmetic. Some also provided industrial school training where pupils were given a basic preparation for the world of work. The West Church schools were erected on the north side of South William Street (between Nelson Street and Princes Street) in 1839 and were described in the *Perthshire Advertiser* as 'plain and handsome' on the outside and spacious and light inside. They were provided with playgrounds, complete with 'swinging poles' for exercise and recreation. On assuming control of the school in the 1870s, the Perth School Board changed its name to Southern District School. It closed in around 1957 with some of the staff transferring to the new Goodlyburn Primary. Prior to demolition in the 1990s, it served briefly as the city's first Further Education Centre and later as an annexe to Perth College. The Middle Church schools followed in 1840 on the west side of Meal Vennel and, in their turn, became Central District School. The development of housing schemes in the suburbs of Perth and the consequent decline in numbers living in the city centre were reflected in a falling school roll, resulting in the school's closure in around 1977 and demolition in the 1980s to allow the

The old Watergate National School, photographed in 1909, several years after it had been replaced by Western District School in Craigie.

construction of the St John's Centre. The East Church schools were in Kinnoull Street, where Knights Court now is.

In a sense, Perth got two church schools for the price of one when, following the Disruption of 1843, the Free Church congregations, not content with building their own new churches, built their own schools as well. The Free West Church school was attached to the church on its northern side and, with access being from North Port, it became known, after its transfer to the School Board, as the North Port School. Its accommodation, however, was below standard by this time and, when plans to transfer it to nearby Blackfriars House fell through, the School Board decided, in 1892, to close it and transfer the pupils to the newly built Caledonian Road School. In its time, though, and within only a few years of its opening, the Free West Church school had earned a reputation

Central District School in Meal Vennel, which was rebuilt in 1902. While Perth may have a somewhat genteel image, the 'gentlemen' sign in the foreground referred to the adjacent public lavatories and not the boys' entrance. Photograph by Tom Berthon, courtesy of Perth Museum and Art Gallery, Perth and Kinross Council.

for the range and quality of its teaching that was surpassed only by that of the Seminaries. Not just the three Rs were taught but English grammar, geography, history, astronomy, mechanics, the sciences, maths, Latin and Greek. Even the esteemed Grammar School had struggled to provide Greek.

Other denominations played their part too. Both Episcopal congregations had small schools attached and the Roman Catholics, whose numbers were already estimated at 500 in 1841, founded St John's School in 1860. Situated approximately where the St John's Centre is today, the school was accessed via a pend from the High Street. George Penny's census of Perth in 1841 also records the existence of a school for the dumb, three dancing schools, seven singing schools and 24 private schools. These last-mentioned establishments were probably little more than spinster or widowed ladies offering lessons in their own homes to a small number of middle- and upper-class pupils.

The sentiments behind the establishment of Perth's bridewell in the tolbooth in the 1830s and the passing of the Poor Law of 1845 were similar to those which led to the founding of industrial schools in Scotland. The guiding principle was to help the (frequently) unemployed poor from drifting into a life of crime by providing basic accommodation and work. The unsuitability of bridewells for the accommodation of children – they were described in the *Perthshire Courier* of 1856 as 'swarming with the unhappy victims of parental neglect' – gave rise to the industrial school movement which focused on orphans and neglected or abused children and provided them with residential accommodation, food, education, religious instruction and training for work.

One of the best known in Perth was the Fechney Industrial School which was founded by the legacy of Mrs Janet Fechney of Ardargie, whose husband had served as lord provost of the city. The school in Spens Crescent, described in a history of the school as a building of 'no architectural pretensions', was opened in 1864 on a 12-acre site which provided wood for heating, vegetables for the dinner table and sufficient grazing for a few cows for milk. In time, it catered for 150 boys, all regarded as destitute on admission and a few verging on the criminal. Outside the schoolroom, the industrial aspect of their education provided the school with a good income. In the workshops, they turned out each week over 115,000 wooden bobbins for the thread manufacturers of Paisley and elsewhere, plus other wooden implements and furniture, and sold large quantities of firewood, specially trimmed to size at a nearby sawmill and split by the boys using a steam-powered machine. There were tailoring and shoe-repair departments, as well as stocking knitting and paper-bag making for local shops. The efficacy of the school was such that, of the 106 boys who had left by 1872, only four were known to have offended.

The Fechney closed in 1922 and the few remaining boys were transferred to Baldovan Industrial School in Dundee. Thereafter, the building was used for a variety of purposes, some industrial and commercial and some connected with wartime activities, but many of a certain age will remember it as the local driving test centre and the place from where they were finally allowed to drive unaccompanied – or not, as the case may have been. When a Japanese businessman finally abandoned his somewhat ambitious plan to dismantle the Fechney stone by stone and ship it to the Far East, it was demolished in 1989.

OVERLEAF. *The Fechney Industrial School with a plentiful supply of timber ready for chopping into firewood.*

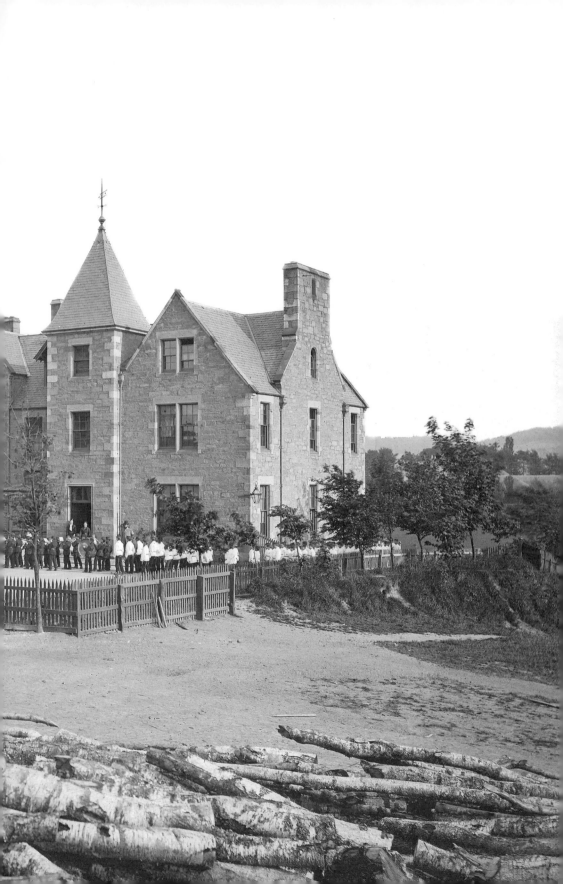

The Fechney School's scout camp in around 1913. Life at the Fechney was not easy but nor was it drudgery. Many former pupils were profoundly grateful for the opportunities and experience the school gave them. Courtesy of the AK Bell Library, Local Studies Department, Perth and Kinross Council

The Fechney's sister institution was the Ladies' House of Refuge for Destitute Girls which was instituted in 1843 and which, under the supervision of a matron, aimed to provide an elementary education and religious instruction to neglected young girls aged between 10 and 14 (the ages were later lowered). Typical of the intake was a girl of 12 whose father was dead and whose alcoholic mother had forced her into thieving. The original home was in Methven Street from where it moved to a location near the waterworks, at the southern end of what is now Tay Street. It had to be given up, though, when the railway was brought across the river at that point, whereupon a new home was found in Craigie.

Opened in what is now Craigieknowes Road in 1856, on a site now occupied by a care home, the new refuge boasted classrooms for basic education, workrooms for acquiring maternal skills and those necessary for life as a housemaid and four bedrooms. The refuge was closed and put up for sale in 1924 at the same time as the Fechney, the remaining girls being transferred to Wellshill Girls Industrial School which had been built adjacent to the

Fechney. Despite the closure of some of these schools, the original trusts continued and were amalgamated into the Perth Homes Trust in 1936. With their combined resources, they purchased Balnacraig in Fairmount Road where, in 1950, the Wellshill girls took up residence.

The twentieth century has witnessed even more school building than the nineteenth, thanks partly to the efforts of the Perth School Board and its successor authorities. The Academy's move to Viewlands was not just a major undertaking in itself but, requiring as it did the removal of a large number of pupils away from the centre of town to the western outskirts, altered the dynamics of the whole city and had a significant impact on the development of the Viewlands area in particular. Similarly distanced from the centre was Perth High School, the city's second senior secondary whose first home at Muirton was then on the northern edge of the city. Its hasty construction in the immediate post-war period gave rise to half a century of problems but they were in the future when Perth High, little more than a collection of prefabs, was opened in 1950. The initial intake comprised the girls of the three-year secondary department of Caledonian Road School and the boys of the three-year secondary department of Balhousie Boys' School which had hitherto provided the secondary education of those pupils who did not proceed to the Academy. The rapidly deteriorating fabric of the school necessitated a further move in 1971 to a brand-new High School at Oakbank, separated from the Academy by little more than the latter's extensive playing fields and Oakbank Primary School. The old school buildings, however, were immediately taken over by Perth's third senior secondary, the newest at that time albeit with the ancient name of Perth Grammar School. The school premises have since been rebuilt.

The story behind the opening in 2010 of Perth's most recent secondary school began with the above-mentioned St John's Roman Catholic Primary. This city-centre school was demolished following the school's removal to a new site in Stormont Street in 1938. Although the Catholic authorities initially opted out of the 1872 Education Act, their schools were absorbed into the state system in the earlier twentieth century and are now classed as denominational schools with a number of rights regarding ethos and worship. The growing numbers at St John's in Stormont Street, junior-secondary pupils as well as primary, prompted the founding, in 1968, of another primary school, Our Lady's, in Letham, and the opening, in 1967, of St Columba's High School in Malvina Place. At the time of writing, the Stormont Street school is about to close and St Columba's has been demolished, both to be replaced by the new St John's Academy, based at the North Inch Community Campus.

Of the city's primary schools, Caledonian Road Primary closed in 2009, the pupils joining the infants of Friarton Nursery to form Inch View Primary on the new Glenearn Community Campus. Northern District Primary dropped its old School Board name and adopted that of Balhousie Primary, an echo of the old Balhousie Boys' School (which closed in 1950 when Perth High was opened) in the Dunkeld Road which is now occupied by St Ninian's Episcopal Primary School. Until around 1977, St Ninian's was part of the nearby Cathedral complex and is the only non-Catholic denominational school in Perth.

Education was never the sole preserve of the Church or the teaching profession. The autodidact enjoys an honourable place in the annals of Scottish learning and many are the stories of self-made men who owed their wealth or achievements in later life to long hours of private study in their youth. For prime examples, one need look no further than the Ettrick Shepherd or emigrant Andrew Carnegie. There are references in the Council minutes of 1723 to the founding of a public library though whether or not this ever materialised is not known to this author. The first one known to have actual books on actual shelves was the Perth Library which was founded by a group of subscribers in 1786 and later opened to all members of the public on payment of an annual subscription. The Rev. Adam Peebles of the qualifying Episcopal congregation was one of the first 'preses of the curators of the Perth Library' which, by the 1790s, was housed in a room in the Session House. This had been allotted to the curators by the Council who seem to have been favourably disposed towards the library's success. When, however, in 1810, this close association resulted in a number of town books being found on the library's shelves, what would be regarded today as a fairly trivial matter was deemed sufficiently serious to merit discussion amongst the magistrates. A measure of the high regard for the Perth Library can be taken from the offer of the subscribers to the Marshall Monument (better known today as the pedimented portico of Perth Museum and Art Gallery) to house the library within its walls and, to this end, the Council, in 1823, granted the Perth Library the substantial sum of 50 guineas as a contribution towards fitting out a room in this prestigious new building. Highly regarded perhaps the library was not widely used. Perth historian Thomas Hay Marshall (no relation, it seems, to his well-known namesake), who made much use of the Perth Library in writing his *History of Perth* in 1849, comments with surprise in the same volume that 'so few of our citizens avail themselves of the privilege within their reach'. And, with 8,000 books on the shelves at that time, mainly historical and philosophical works, it was indeed a well-stocked though perhaps narrowly focused collection. Even so, a published list of additions to the library in the period between 1849 and 1856 shows that popular items such as *David Copperfield, Vanity Fair, Uncle Tom's Cabin* and *Coningsby* were all available, as were biographies and books on travel, local history and topics of the day such as animal magnetism.

With an annual subscription in 1849 of 11 shillings, the Perth Library was, in practice, only open to those of reasonable means. To cater for the city's less well-off residents, the Perth Mechanics' Reading Society was established in 1823 and within 25 years had a stock of 3,000 volumes, available to members at a weekly subscription of only a penny. The society suffered a disastrous fire in 1869 when its entire stock of 7,000 volumes went up in flames but the premises were rebuilt and the books replaced. Prior to the fire, the library was housed, at one stage, in the Hammermen's Hall in a pend off the High Street (just to the east of what is now Perth Theatre) and, latterly, at South St John's Place. To quote the *Perthshire Advertiser* of 1926, it was largely due to the influence of the Mechanics' Library that 'the operatives and mechanics in the city gained the reputation of unusual intelligence and mental accomplishment'. These two main publicly available resources were complemented by the libraries of many local churches, such as the North United Presbyterian Congregation (the North Church today) whose published catalogue of 1864 lists many theological and improving items as well as volumes of poetry and fiction and books about history and the sciences. Others included the Perth Public Library which was founded in around 1809 and later became the Perth Reading Society, the Perth Students' Union, the Co-operative Library (in Scott Street) and an institution known as Drummond's Library which was founded by writer and bookseller P. R. Drummond and described by George Penny in 1841 as 'a splendid collection' of books which could be borrowed 'by the year, half year, quarter, or by the night'. There may have been libraries in schools too but not in Perth's two National Schools, the teachers of which petitioned both the Council and the government in 1839 for a contribution towards establishing a library but were turned down by both.

Two further institutions of note were the Bridgend Institute established in 1878 in Strathmore Street, on a site now occupied by sheltered housing, and the Victoria Institute which stood on the south side of Jeanfield Road, a little to the east of Spens Crescent. The latter was first proposed in 1886 and was considerably helped to fruition by the generosity of the Caledonian Railway which provided the land at a nominal rent. Victoria's Golden Jubilee celebrations in 1887 added a sense of occasion to the laying of the foundation stone and presumably also the name. The institute survived until waning interest in the mid 1960s forced its closure and subsequent sale.

Perth's first free public library was established by the will of Professor

The Bridgend Institute in Strathmore Street in 1908.

Archibald Sandeman who died in 1893, bequeathing the residue of his estate – some £30,000 – to the Council for the purpose of founding a free library in the city. The foundation stone was laid in October 1896 by Lord Provost John Dewar and, two years later, almost to the day, the dominant building of Kinnoull Street was opened by former premier Lord Rosebery who, at the same time, was presented with the freedom of the burgh. Most of the other libraries in Perth at that time willingly supported the new venture – in 1897, the directors of the old Mechanics' Library, seemingly now moribund, gave their collection of around 11,000 volumes, valued at c. £1,000, to the Council with a view to them being used in the new library and one or two others did the same. Even today, it is possible to find a few books in the special collec-

The opening of the Sandeman Public Library in 1898. Judging by the body language of those waiting, Lord Rosebery appears to have been a little late.

tions of the AK Bell Library stamped with the name of the Perth Mechanics' Institute. The top floor of the library housed the city's first proper art gallery, a comfortably furnished and well-lit room though, with so many stairs to climb, the difficulties of access must have been a deterrent to some. When the new art gallery opened in 1935, as an extension to the museum in George Street, the room was vacated and later served as a library store and later still a local studies centre.

The Sandeman quickly carved a role for itself in the hearts and minds of the Perth public – so much so that a somewhat utilitarian extension had to be built in the 1930s. The expansion of services continued under a succession of city librarians until, in 1972, the long-discussed merger of the city and county

The top floor of the Sandeman Library housed an art gallery which, in its time, hosted some important exhibitions.

library services was finally completed. By the early 1980s, the Sandeman building was becoming inadequate for the use being made of it and it closed in 1994, after almost a century of service to the Perth public. Some years after the opening of its successor, the AK Bell Library in York Place, the Sandeman became a pub. Up to the end, though, the first-floor reference and reading room, with its archways, high ceiling and oak tables, was where generations of senior pupils and students studied quietly for exams – and where younger ones, lurking behind pillars beyond the librarian's stare, first sniggered over dictionary definitions of *mauvais mots*.

Academic interests in Perth found an outlet through the city's learned societies of which the first to be established, at the suggestion of local minister James Scott, was the Antiquarian Society in 1784 (renamed as the Literary and Antiquarian Society in 1786). The principal aims initially were the study of Scottish and local history, later broadened to include other disciplines. The society had a library which, by 1850, could boast items as disparate as a Koran, a Chinese Bible, an Irish grammar and a volume of Serbian poetry. The society also had an extensive museum collection and, like the Perth Library, took up the offer to house it in part of the Marshall Monument. It seems that the museum collection there was sufficiently widely known and well regarded to merit the donation in 1841 of John Knox's walking stick (or so it was claimed at the time) from a well-wisher in London. The society is absent from the listings in the *Perth Directory* after 1913 and was presumably wound up on the outbreak of war. In 1914, the Monument and its collections were taken over by the Council and became the nucleus of the present museum collection. And, yes, the walking stick is still there.

The Council had earlier, in 1903, accepted the gift of the museum building at 66 Tay Street, which belonged to the Perthshire Society of Natural Science, together with the exhibits therein. Despite the change in ownership, the museum continued to function in Tay Street until the newly extended Perth Museum and Art Gallery in George Street opened in 1935, whereupon the Tay Street museum was closed and the collection transferred to the new building. The society was founded in 1867 and, at the time of writing, is approaching its 150th anniversary.

A third learned society, the Andersonian Institution, named after the highly regarded Academy rector Adam Anderson, was more scientific in interests and catered mainly to the working and middle classes. It too had a library of several hundred volumes. The institution hosted a series of lectures in the Guild Hall in the 1850s on subjects as varied as fine arts, music, civil engineering and animal magnetism. However, what the audience made of 'Vegetable Physiology as Illustrative of the Unity of the Godhead' – apparently an argument that the existence of God, and one God only, could be proven by the structure of plants and flowers – is unrecorded.

Although not as widely patronised as some writers might have wished, the libraries and learned societies of Perth together with the Academy's long and proud scholastic history gave Perth a reputation as one of the more educated cities of Scotland. Add to this the output of the Morison family's printing presses and a flowering of Georgian architecture and Perth should be regarded as a town of significance within the story of the Scottish Enlightenment.

CHAPTER 9

SPORT AND LEISURE
IN OLD PERTH

The highpoint of the city's sporting calendar was the annual Perth races which were eagerly anticipated by all ages and levels of society – from schoolchildren to the elderly, from tricksters to magistrates, from farm workers and shop girls to noble lords and gentrified ladies. Punters and publicans, and others who stood to gain more than most from the celebratory mood, would have had the dates noted in their diaries for months. Accounts from the 1830s describe how children rushed out of school at 4.00 p.m. on race days (from 1850 classes were permitted to finish at 1.00 p.m. on such occasions), heading for the North Inch to admire the horses and swelling the already large crowds of townspeople, augmented by visitors and gentry from Perthshire and neighbouring counties. The gentlemen of the Perth Hunt were in charge, having taken over the organisation of the races from the Council in 1784, and were usually seen busily gathered around the steward's box, leaving their wives and ladies safely ensconced in the grandstand which was built for the occasion each year beside the river, facing towards Rose Terrace. The actual races, it seems, were held in a clockwise direction which is apparently unusual nowadays but perhaps not so then. Rival attractions to the on-course events were fruit sellers, musicians – pipers, fiddlers and singers – and hawkers selling gewgaws and trinkets. Most popular, though, were the refreshment tents, numbering as many as 50, which occupied the area between the south end of the Inch and the winning post at the grandstand. Many Perth publicans erected their own tents, with bar and seating inside, and served whisky by the gill glass (equivalent to four or five pub measures today) to thronging customers. In the evening, long after the races had finished for the day, lamps were lit and the drinking went on until late at night. Fights broke out, some real and some fake, the latter staged to attract curious spectators who immediately and professionally had their pockets picked. Pranks were played, sometimes by mischievous schoolboys who hung around

There is no documentation accompanying this photograph but it is thought to be a scene at Perth Races on the North Inch. The roof of the grandstand can be made out in the background, centre-right.

outside the tents waiting for an unsuspecting drinker on the inside to touch the tent wall, whereupon his arm was given a sharp shove and his whisky sent flying. Police were in attendance during the day but it seems their principal duty was to keep the racetrack clear. In the 1840s, the magistrates took the first steps to regulate the opening hours of the refreshment tents but they were made somewhat ineffective by enterprising liquor dealers who, for a short period at least, managed to evade the restrictions by hiring boats and supplying whisky from the river instead. Meanwhile, the ladies and gentlemen and gentry and nobility of the Perth Hunt, eschewing the bibulous crowds on the Inch, would perhaps have adjourned to the theatre for a show before gathering in the ballrooms of County Buildings and the main inns of the town for reels and dancing (perhaps to the music of Niel Gow or Samson Duncan) and food and speeches. Later, according to the press, in the early hours of a new day, the hardier carousers moved on to the George Inn for 'grilled bones' and punch and, thus fortified, set off with the foxhounds in the morning.

A newspaper account of the 1858 races focused rather more on the off-course activities, particularly of the out-of-town 'thimblers' who, armed with three thimbles, an upturned barrel and a pea, invited locals to bet on which thimble was hiding the aforesaid legume. It was, of course, an old trick and the newspaper first expressed surprise that anyone could still fall for such a commonplace display of sleight of hand. Then came the story of how, at the start of the second day's racing, the townspeople suddenly turned on the thimblers and threw their barrels and other appurtenances into the Tay and how, at the end of the day, they planned an attack on the stall holders at the foot of the Inch. When the signal was given, the crowd overthrew their tables, trampling goods underfoot and sending others flying through the air to the extent that 'nuts, toys, sweeties, apples, accordions, penny jewellery etc. were showering about like hail or grapeshot'. Such levels of violence were far from uncommon in old Perth.

The first reference to racing appears in the Council minutes of 1613, when a silver bell was awarded to the winner of a race around the South Inch. In the mid seventeenth century, racing was transferred to the North Inch where the oblong shape of the track was judged to be fairer to all horses than the rounder one of its former home. Later, in order to double – almost – the length of the straights of the North Inch course, a couple of gaps were temporarily knocked through the White Dyke, which marked the boundary between town lands and those of the Earl of Kinnoull, thereby increasing the course to a length close to that of the circumferential path of today. The Council continued to sponsor the races until 1833 through the provision of a valuable cup or plate as a prize though, on occasions, having presumably witnessed the galling spectacle of a single horse and rider strolling around the course before walking off with their silverware, they specified that at least two horses should have to compete for any prize they offered.

The Caledonian Hunt made regular visits to the city, the last one being in 1890 when the rain was torrential and the river so full that water was almost lapping the edge of the track. It seems, though, that the condition of the course itself, rather than the weather, was the reason for its abandonment as, a couple of years later, the Jockey Club forbade any further flat racing on the North Inch under its rules. Racing continued under alternative rules until around 1908 when the 5th Earl of Mansfield invited the races to the grounds of Scone Palace where they have been ever since. The earl's grandfather, the fourth earl, who died in 1898, was also a keen supporter of the races and would invariably cause a stir by arriving on the North Inch in his boat carriage which was basically a horse-drawn rowing boat on wheels. It all added to the spectacle that was the Perth Races.

Almost as big a sporting occasion on the North Inch was the cricket fixture between local rivals, Perthshire and Forfarshire. Cricket was historically considered to be Perth's game – so much so that, when local suffragettes wished to strike a blow of freedom against the Perthshire male, they chose to burn down the cricket pavilion on the North Inch rather than, say, the St Johnstone stand near the South Inch. The first recorded game in Perth was on the North Inch in around 1812 and, within 15 years, the Perth (later Perthshire) Cricket Club had been formed. The 1890s were a particularly successful period for the club but could not compare with the period between 1953 and 1978 when Perthshire won the Scottish Counties Championship an unmatched total of 20 times. Up to the outbreak of World War II, Perthshire's games on the North Inch – particularly when playing Forfarshire – could attract crowds of several thousand though, oddly enough, spectator numbers began to dwindle just as the players were achieving their greatest successes. After 1978, Perthshire began a long and dizzying fall from grace, plummeting from Scottish county champions to relegation from the national cricket league in less than 30 years. Cricket is still played on the North Inch though only in front of a relatively small number of spectators.

In August 1903, when Perthshire was enjoying some success on the pitch, disaster struck in the grandstand. Just over half full with 600 seated spectators, the 50-metre-long stand suddenly collapsed, injuring many, including the widow of Arthur Bell of the whisky firm. Her son, A.K. Bell, was a keen cricketer and may possibly have been there too. Cabs and carriages queued up on the pitch to ferry the injured to hospital and the streets between the Inch and the York Place infirmary were reportedly lined with anxious family members scanning each vehicle for loved ones. There were no fatalities though it took Perthshire several years to pay off all the claims for damages.

The popularity of cricket in the later nineteenth century is reckoned to have delayed the arrival of association football in the city, if only by a few years. Football had been played in Perth for centuries and probably according to rules, if any there were, that had been agreed just before the start of a game. Most books about football in Perth mention the great match which took place on the North Inch in 1836 and it is worth recounting the details if only to contrast the old game with that of today. It all began at the annual dinner of the Literary and Antiquarian Society in November 1835 when, in the course of his speech, Lord Stormont mentioned his regret at the passing of the ancient Scottish games which used to be played on the North Inch. In reply, Lord Provost Adam Pringle challenged him to a Perth versus Scone football match, 50-a-side, with peer and provost playing against each other. Described in the

A cricket match on the North Inch when spectators were in sufficient numbers to warrant a grandstand. The bandstand can be seen behind it.

press as the biggest clash on the North Inch since the Battle of the Clans in 1396, the two teams stepped out on Handsel Monday, 8 January 1836, in front of a crowd estimated at 14,000. The majority seem to have been Perth supporters who were quick to get behind their team – and not only behind but in front too, so much so that, there being no attempt at crowd control, the Scone team quickly found that they could hardly see the ball, let alone work out who was a player and who a spectator. The game was abandoned and declared a draw. At the post-match dinner for the Scone team, Lord Stormont proposed a toast to 'the Lord Provost of Perth, and when we next go to play football with him, may his arrangements for keeping a clear field be efficient and complete'. The Scone players, however, were rather less gentle in their criticism, as is demonstrated by a letter to the press: 'The disgraceful usage we received at the end was the worst of the whole. We were followed down the Inch by a mob of disorderly persons, pelting us with stones and turf, and using the most abusive language to us, till we were obliged to take refuge . . . This all happened without the smallest effort on the part of the Perth authorities to prevent this disorder. To be abused in this way, after meeting the Perth people on their own ground . . . must certainly appear to every person most unhandsome conduct; and it will be a deep stain on the character of the "Fair City".' He concluded by saying they would be happy to play Perth again but – damningly – not within eight miles of the city.

Association football, rather better regulated, arrived in Perth in around 1884 when several teams were started up, generally by sportsmen such as cricketers or rowers who had experienced the game elsewhere and suggested it as an activity for the winter months. In quick succession came Fair City Athletic Football Club (originally cricketers), Pullars Rangers (rowers), Erin Rovers (mainly those of Irish descent) and St Johnstone (again originally cricketers). The Inches were the obvious place to play but a combination of heavy boots, weighty footballs and winter rain churned up the turf so much that the Council made its first attempt to ban football on the Inches as early as March 1885. The clubs, numbering 39 by November 1887, regularly petitioned the Council to be allowed to play, with limited success, but it quickly became clear to the senior clubs that they would need to find grounds of their own. Thus Fair City Athletic first hired a curling pond at Hillyland and then grounds in the Dunkeld Road from which they were shortly evicted to make way for the new swimming baths. Pullars Rangers, later renamed Caledonian Rangers because of the connection of a number of players with the Caledonian Railway, used railway ground at Feus Wynd (later lengthened and renamed Feus Road) which was known as Caledonian Park. The club disbanded in around 1890 when the railway wanted the ground back. Erin Rovers, which disbanded at around the same time due to financial problems, played at St Catherine's Park, sandwiched between the lade and the Wallace Works. The only senior Perth club to survive those initial years was St Johnstone which leased ground at Craigie Haugh (opposite the entrance to Perth Prison) from Sir Robert Moncreiffe. St Johnstone Park, as it was later known, was opened in August

An 1880s photograph of the earliest days of St Johnstone FC. Despite the bats and pads, the trophy was apparently awarded for success on the football pitch. Courtesy of the AK Bell Library, Local Studies Department, Perth and Kinross Council

1885 and, with its pavilion, was regarded as one of the best grounds in the north.

The steady advance of Saints through the ranks of Scottish football resulted in attendances of 10,000 or more by the 1920s and there was a consequent need for better accommodation. Thanks to the Earl of Mansfield's offer of land at South Muirton, the club, on the verge of promotion to the first division, were able to move into Muirton Park where the first game was played on Christmas Day 1924. And there they stayed, through good seasons and some very bad, until the 1980s when numbers in the stands had to be limited because of their poor condition (the stands, that is, not the supporters). At the end of that decade there fell into place a complex deal between the club, the neighbouring ice rink (which later dropped out), local farmer Bruce McDiarmid and supermarket chain Asda, which resulted in Asda buying Muirton Park and building a brand new all-seater stadium on the edge of town at the Crieff Road, on land that had been virtually given to the club by McDiarmid. Only when the new stadium was ready were Asda were permitted to demolish Muirton Park and build the supermarket that is still there today.

Like cricket, the fair-weather sport of rowing had also indirectly contributed to the rise of winter football. The rowers of Perth in the nineteenth century had seen – perhaps rather more clearly than we do today – that the Tay upstream of Perth Bridge, with its straight course and wide, smooth and generally gentle flow, was ideal for rowing contests. There are references to boat races on the Tay as far back as 1827 though the first regattas were held nearer the harbour, running between Friarton and the mouth of the Earn and back again. By the second half of the century, rowing had become a popular spectator sport and was now taking place further upstream where people could watch. The *Perthshire Courier* described how the 1868 season got underway with a 'grand aquatic procession' which filled the river between Perth Bridge and the Springland tower with craft of all kinds. There was even a small steamer from Dundee – the first time such a vessel had been seen opposite the North Inch. Five years later, according to the same newspaper, Perth Rowing Club and City of Perth Rowing Club raced between Boatland House and 'the old bottle works' at the shore and back again, finishing opposite the fishing lodge on the North Inch. City of Perth, in *Raven*, began strongly and, achieving a rate of 49 strokes per minute, attempted to take the opposition's water by going through their designated arch of Perth Bridge. But Perth, in *Bonnie Lass*, managed to hold on and forced City at the last minute to revert to their own arch, an act which cost them valuable time and ultimately the race. Perth Rowing Club both celebrated the win and rubbed salt into City's wounds by launching a new pleasure boat which was named *The Victory*. The *Bonnie Lass* was still doing well in regattas a number of years later.

Paddle-steamer trips along the Tay between Perth and Dundee were a relaxing pastime for many and even led to the publication of a guidebook, *The Steamboat Companion betwixt Perth and Dundee*, in 1838. The dictates of the tide, however, combined with the speed of the vessel, allowed passengers arriving at Perth only a matter of minutes before they had to reboard for the two-hour voyage back to Dundee. And arriving as they did at the Lime Shore (occasionally the tide allowed the vessel to travel further upstream), there was not a great deal there to amuse them. All that changed with the launch of the *Lass o' Gowrie* in 1841 which allowed two hours in the Fair City before the return journey, plenty of time for refreshment or a stroll around the Inches. *Cleopatra*, which was broken up in the 1930s, also paddled along the Perth–

Under the shadow of Kinnoull Hill, the paddle steamer Cleopatra *begins her journey down the Tay to Dundee.*

Dundee route, as did the *Dundee*, which was still operating in the 1920s, if not later, between Broughty Ferry, Dundee and Perth. McGonagall gives an insight into pleasure trips on the Tay in a poem recounting the unfortunate end to an earlier incarnation of the *Dundee* in 1888:

> an alarming accident occurred in the River Tay
> which resulted in the sinking of the Tay Ferries' steamer *Dundee*
> which was a most painful and sickening sight to see.

The day ended reasonably happily when,

> thanks be to God, all the passengers were sent to Dundee
> by the steamers *Renown, Forfarshire, Protector*, and the *Lass o' Gowrie*,
> which certainly was a most beautiful sight to see,
> when they landed 900 passengers safe on the pier at Dundee.

Quite a disaster – as was, of course, the sinking of the steamer . . .
  Competitive rowing and steamer trips were joined at the century's end by

the rather more simple pleasure of pootling about in a hired rowing boat, courtesy of the boat station just upstream of Perth Bridge. When, however, the operator found he could make little profit from the boats they were withdrawn in around 1981.

Swimming as a sport was becoming more popular throughout the country in the second half of the nineteenth century and was, no doubt, boosted by the daring Channel-swimming exploits of Captain Matthew Webb in 1875. A swimming pool for the city was first proposed in around 1880 but rejected in favour of improving the baths and wash house in Mill Street. Later, thanks to the initiative and hard work of Robert Pullar, the necessary funds were raised by subscription and, in the spring of 1889, the swimming baths were opened on a site on the Dunkeld Road where the Royal Bank of Scotland now is. The building, according to the *Perthshire Courier*'s account of its opening, initially contained two pools though there was the intention to add Turkish baths later, 'to bring Perth up to the level of the other cities of the Empire'. Water, heated, was supplied from the lade and the prevailing decor was a rather exotic terracotta.

From its earliest days, though, there was a widespread feeling that the baths were too far from the city centre and, when refurbishment was required in the 1930s – owing partly to the vast numbers of schoolchildren now using the establishment who, said the *Perthshire Advertiser*, were packed in 'like herring in a barrel' – a number of councillors took the opportunity to press for new baths closer to the centre. Sites near the City Mills, the new Art Gallery and even in the High Street were all mentioned as alternatives but, along with proposals for an open-air pool, were rejected in favour of reconstruction and extension on the same spot.

The improved baths were reopened in 1937, complete with a large new pool built over the site of the Corporation bowling green. The pavilion-esque entrance hall at the front, with separate entrances for men and women, was removed to allow space for a car park and a single sex entrance was instead formed at the side. Inside, the former ladies' pool was made shallower and converted into a children's pool. The main pool was extended to championship length in 1962 thus making it one of the premier competition pools in Scotland, and was even fitted up to take television cameras.

By the early 1970s, though, the nineteenth-century building was falling far short of twentieth-century standards. In response to letters in the press about

OVERLEAF. *As with rowing regattas and paddle steamers, the North Inch boat station, photographed in 1910, has also gone from the river.*

The swimming baths were initially inviting and attractive in appearance. During the twentieth century, the significant improvements to the indoor facilities were inversely matched by the deteriorating outward aspect, a process hastened by the removal of the entrance pavilion.

cold temperatures and primitive changing conditions, the Council took the major decision in 1982 to build what is now the Perth Leisure Pool on former railway land at Glover Street, having rejected two other front-running sites on the South Inch. And, although probably no nearer the town centre than the old baths, it is at least no longer at the edge of town.

Another water-based sport was curling which was played in Perth certainly as early as the seventeenth century. It was a relatively inexpensive activity and, perhaps for this reason, there were a number of curling ponds in and around the city in the nineteenth century. One was created in 1840 a little to the north of the North Inch by unemployed workers on a job creation scheme and its hollow is still visible from the adjacent footpath. The small cutting beside the golf course near the top of the North Inch was dug at the

An interior view of Perth Swimming Baths on the Dunkeld Road. This was latterly known as the Soldiers' Pool and some Perth residents will remember the changing cubicles at the side.

same time to allow water to drain from the pond into the river. Three years later both the Perth Curling Club and the St John's Curling Club successfully petitioned the Council for space to form ponds on the South Inch. Other ponds were made at Maggie's Park, Hillyland and Gannochy, all of which have long since disappeared though the green space of the last-mentioned is still known locally as the Curly. In the winter of 1895, one of the coldest on record, the Tay at Perth froze to such a depth that curling and skating were enjoyed for several weeks. A great bonspiel was held in February opposite the upper end of the North Inch while, further downstream at County Buildings, the ice had to be dynamited at the start of the fishing season.

Around forty years later, in 1936, Perth's first indoor ice rink was opened on a site in the Dunkeld Road adjacent to Muirton Park. Aimed at the curlers of Perthshire, Angus, Fife and Kinross-shire, it was appropriately named the Central Scotland Ice Rink and was regarded as a focus for the nation's winter sports, this being a time when ski-ing in Scotland was for the few who had transport to the still-undeveloped slopes. As well as curling and skating the new rink also gave a boost to ice hockey which, according to the press at the time, had hitherto only been played outdoors on frozen ponds with upturned walking sticks. It quickly became a popular spectator sport at the rink where the Perth public could enjoy the speed and skill of two top-class local teams, the Perth Panthers and the Perth Black Hawks, though their strengths were somewhat enhanced by a number of Canadian professionals. Some of the players were on a par with Hollywood film stars in the dreams of Perth's teenage girls.

The rink was judged to be extremely successful in its time, bringing to Perth the excitement of ice hockey and world-class curling. It was extended on occasions and later included facilities for squash and indoor bowling. By the later 1980s, though, like its neighbour, Muirton Park, the ice rink was showing its age and, at around the time St Johnstone moved out to McDiarmid Park, it too moved to brand-new premises at the Dewars Centre, on the site of the whisky firm's recently demolished bonded warehouse. The old rink was demolished in 1990.

The principal places of resort for the social classes who did not attend society balls or dinners were the city's many public houses. Indeed, prior to the nineteenth century and apart from early theatres, public houses would have provided the only indoor leisure space for the great mass of townspeople. Little wonder, then, that church ministers and others who saw the damage that excessive alcohol consumption could inflict bemoaned what they regarded as far too many pubs in town. To quote the local minister who, in 1837, wrote the Perth chapter in the *New Statistical Account*, 'In the public streets, and in the private lanes and closes, there are small tippling houses in which tippling is carried on to a fearful extent . . . [and] to the existence of these houses may be easily traced the poverty and domestic wretchedness of many a family.' The council minutes record the very public descent into poverty of 'Mr Hamilton', a teacher of English at the Seminaries, who, in January 1840, had been seen in various public houses in the city, drinking whisky and porter and conversing with women 'of bad fame'. He was then seen entering a house 'usually resorted to by profligate characters of both sexes' where he drank more and apparently partook in 'indecent liberties and familiarities' with two women, one of whom then proceeded to rob him of a watch. The case came to court and, when the details became public knowledge, Hamilton was regarded as an unsuitable

The bitterly cold winter of 1895, when the Tay froze to such a depth that curling, skating and even horse-drawn sleigh rides were enjoyed. Courtesy of the AK Bell Library, Local Studies Department, Perth and Kinross Council

character to be a teacher at the Seminaries and was dismissed. Three months later, he applied to be admitted to the poor roll.

Pubs and prostitution not infrequently went together, particularly in the South Street area which was known for both. But there were higher classes of inns too, such as, of course, the George Inn, which at very short notice, in 1848, hosted the queen and Prince Albert who were journeying south from Balmoral. George Penny, in his census of Perth of 1841, distinguished four types of drinking establishment: inns, of which there were eight; 'respectable taverns', ten; 'public houses with stabling', fifty-six; and 'tippling houses', ninety-nine. This may sound a lot but it was a considerable reduction on the 400 tippling houses in 1830, mentioned in connection with a proposed Licensing Act. One third of these had apparently been started up in the previous five years.

The tightening grip of the Church on society in the second half of the nineteenth century is reflected in a mass petition of townspeople to the Council – signed by 2,253 people – to restrict the number of pubs in the city. It was

The Kinnoull Arms in South Methven Street in the 1930s, one of perhaps rather too many drinking establishments in Perth – at least, according to the authorities and temperance campaigners.

further demonstrated by the formation of temperance societies, petitions against certain pubs being granted a licence (occasionally counter-petitioned by customers who wanted the licence to be retained), petitions against Sunday drinking and moves to prevent the sale of alcohol on Council-owned property. Even in recent years, the press has featured comments about the excessive number of pubs in the city centre – a figure described in 1998 as well above the Scottish average.

Several Perth pubs were mentioned in an 1805 advertisement for a theatre show and included the Black Lion, Red Lion, White Lion, Golden Lion, Thistle and Crown, Nag's Head, Black Bull, White Bull, Black Cow, Highlander, Swan, Pack Horse, Turk's Head, Boar's Head, Plough and Horse, Horse and Gig, Horse and Traveller and three which are still in existence today, the George, Salutation and the Ship. One of the most famous of Perth pubs was the King's Arms which was accessed from the Cunningham Graham Close at the foot of the High Street. The building itself, once the premier public house of Perth which enjoyed the patronage of the Duke of Atholl, was purchased by the Conservative Club in 1892 and subsequently demolished to make way for an extension to their clubrooms in George Street. The reopening of another, the Parliament Bar, was announced in the press of 1840 in the following terms: 'Donald Menzies begs to intimate that he has opened that long-established and well-frequented tavern in the Parliament Close, High Street, and hopes, by strict attention to business, and moderate charges, to merit a share of public patronage. The house has recently been fitted up with hot, cold and shower baths, on the most approved principles, and gentlemen may have the use of them at a low rate. The stabling and other accommodation is extensive and commodious.'

Apart from pubs, there were also coffee rooms which seemed to serve as gentlemen's private clubs, making newspapers and periodicals – such as the London *Times* and the *Perthshire Courier* – available to members and providing indoor space for the transaction of business, the discussion of the latest news from London and the exchange of local gossip. Prime amongst them were the Exchange Coffee Rooms in George Street. They seem to have declined in popularity in the later nineteenth century, their function perhaps being replaced by Liberal and Conservative clubrooms which opened in George Street in the 1880s. Indeed, the Liberals' second set of clubrooms were established in the old coffee rooms in 1889. There were also temperance and working men's coffee rooms in the city and, as previously mentioned, several reading rooms and social institutes.

Drama in Perth goes back to at least the sixteenth century with a performance of Sir David Lindsay's *Ane Pleasant Satyre of the Thrie Estaitis* at an open-air amphitheatre near today's Rosslyn House, in front of James V. Performances of St Obert's Play, in honour of the rather obscure patron saint of the Baker Incorporation, may go back even further (the play was banned by the Kirk Session in 1581). Regular theatrical performances took place in the Guild Hall in the High Street for much of the eighteenth century, until 1786 when the Glovers' Hall was erected in George Street and fitted out as a theatre of sorts. *The Siege of Perth* was performed there in 1792 and proved to be one of the most popular plays of its time. What literally brought the house down, though, was a performance of *Macbeth* in 1809 during which the gallery crashed down on the audience below, injuring many. Thereafter, the old Grammar School in St Ann's Lane, vacant since 1807, was converted into a

theatre and leased out by the Council. It opened in 1810 and over the ensuing ten years, thanks to well-known thespians such as Mr and Mrs Henry Siddons (Henry being the son of the famous Sarah) and Corbet Ryder who took the lease, the theatre became immensely popular, often drawing heaving crowds to the narrow confines of St Ann's Lane, desperate to get in for the evening's performance. One particularly popular production was *Rob Roy*, a dramatisation of Scott's novel of 1817, which was first put on at Covent Garden in March 1818, where it ran for some considerable time, before coming to Perth in June of that year. Despite some negative comments about accents, such as that repeated in Peter Baxter's *Drama in Perth* – 'Mr Johnson as Rob Roy (although a favourite actor) would have appeared to better advantage had he been a little more conversant with the Scottish dialect' – the play ran and ran. Ryder tried on several occasions to give other plays an airing but demand for *Rob Roy* was so high that it was performed at Perth on well over one hundred occasions.

A view of the short-lived Opera House on the corner of Canal Street and Tay Street. Whatever the Council's opinion on this perceived threat to the City Hall, they could hardly fault the architectural addition to their showcase street.

Ryder's lease ended in 1819 whereupon he moved to Aberdeen. The old Grammar School theatre remained empty for a few years and was then destroyed by fire. Meanwhile, through the efforts of Sir David Moncreiffe, a keen patron of local drama, a handsome new theatre had been built at the corner of Atholl Street and Kinnoull Street (now a restaurant) which opened in 1820 as the Theatre Royal. Ryder was quickly attracted back to Perth but the new theatre was never as successful as the old and by 1825 the shareholders were giving serious consideration to selling it. However, in the midst of a succession of dismal seasons, the long-remembered visit of Paganini stands out. He performed at the Theatre Royal in 1831, an occasion which has been described as the greatest musical event in the history of Perth and, in terms of the impact he had, that probably still holds true. But not even the maestro could mitigate the effects of cholera on theatre attendances in the 1830s or the virtual abandonment of the theatre in the later 1840s following the opening of the City Hall. The Theatre Royal, which began with such high hopes, was sold in 1860 for a fraction of its original building cost and converted into a clothing store.

Plays and theatrical performances were, thereafter, held in the City Hall, though there are occasional references in the local press to other short-lived playhouses. One, mentioned in the *Perthshire Courier*, opened in Canal Street in the later 1820s but did not long survive calls for its closure on the grounds of it being 'an illegal and immoral establishment'. Injuries caused to the audience when a gallery collapsed did not help matters. Eventually, as the press noted, '[T]he actors were forcibly transferred from the hall in Canal Street to a more modest apartment in the Police Office. In court they pleaded their case and were dismissed on condition that the theatre was closed.'

In 1879, the very obvious shortcomings of the City Hall led to a proposal by Robert Pullar to build a new privately funded public hall. The prospectus issued at the time argued that it would be impossible to make the City Hall 'comfortable for any purpose of meeting whatever' but this did not prevent the Council from trying. To counter such a direct threat to their ageing showpiece hall, they commissioned a survey which, perhaps to their chagrin, seemed to accept the points made by the Pullar party. As a consequence of the survey, however, a number of improvements were carried out over the next few years and the City Hall limped along for almost another three decades. The new public hall, built in Scottish baronial style on a prime site at the corner of Tay Street and Canal Street, with its main entrance looking towards County Buildings, was opened in March 1881 and, in grandeur, mirrored the recently completed Municipal Buildings on the northern corner of Tay Street and High Street. The first event was a performance of *Messiah* which featured the combined talents of two choirs accompanied by Perth Amateur Orchestra. A description of the interior, with gallery, proscenium, raked flooring, ventilation and comfortable arm chairs with lifting seats, as well as additional smaller halls, cloakrooms, lavatories, a kitchen and space for an organ, shows very clearly that it was designed to serve the functions of a city hall and theatre combined. Perhaps the only drawback was that it could hold only 1,055 people as opposed to the 1,800 of the City Hall.

Despite its lavish furnishings, the new hall was not a great success. Initially it housed a gymnasium before becoming far better known from the mid 1880s as the Perth Opera House. But even this did not last long and the building was sold in 1891 for less than half the original building cost a mere ten

Free St Leonard's Church in Victoria Street which was later adapted to a roller-skating rink, a cinema and a bingo hall. What would that church's first minister have thought?

years or so earlier. The performance of the last opera, *The Gondoliers,* given by D'Oyly Carte on Saturday 30 May 1891, was a glittering occasion. The orchestra was augmented by professionals, the scenery and costumes were magnificent and hundreds had to be turned away at the door. The new owners, the Perth Baptist congregation, remained in occupancy until the building was destroyed in a major conflagration in July 1984.

Theatre was resurrected in Perth in 1900 with the opening of the present High Street building, where, with another extension currently underway, it continues to flourish. Another theatre, the Pavilion, opened in 1928 on the South Inch, at the junction of Marshall Place and the Edinburgh Road. Less serious in intent than its High Street counterpart – more Harry Lauder than *Henry V* – it aimed to put on twice-nightly summer variety shows, particularly for visitors to the city. In the aftermath of World War II, it became a transport café and was demolished in around 1973.

The Star Picture House in 1918, formerly the Corona, which was housed beneath the Guild Hall in the High Street.

In tandem with the story of Perth Theatre went that of the city's several picture houses. Cinematography, the latest development in the rapidly evolving world of photography, arrived in Perth at around the turn of the century where the earliest films were probably shown in the first City Hall. One show there was announced for December 1902 when events making the news were to be projected on to a screen. Recent film shows had featured the visit of the German emperor to the United Kingdom and the departure of Mr and Mrs Joseph Chamberlain for South Africa. Elsewhere in town, the earliest cinemas were generally shops which had been converted with little difficulty into small and basic picture houses.

The first major conversion of a large building into a cinema was that of the old Free St Leonard's Church in Victoria Street. Following the opening of a new church in Marshall Place (now St Leonard's-in-the-Fields), the old church had become first a furniture store, then the Victoria Skating Rink (for roller skating) and then a cinema attached to the B.B. chain (this being an abbreviation for Bright and Beautiful), one of several in Scotland. It was fairly basic and, with its wooden benches, not particularly comfortable though this all changed following a serious fire in 1922. The cinema was quickly rebuilt and partially remodelled and, when it reopened in 1923, was equipped with better tip-up seating on two levels, an orchestra pit, central heating and ventilation and, perhaps most importantly, fire extinguishing equipment and fire exits. The B.B. in time became the Cinerama before converting to a bingo hall in 1962. It was demolished in recent years.

The Corona Picture House, later the Star, opened in 1913. Described in the press as 'this most artistic building in the High Street', it had smoke-free accommodation for 200 and showed three different films each week. The entrance was brilliantly lit with electric light and must have been an attractive feature of the street at night. The Magnet Picture Palace opened in Scott Street in around 1912 and closed in 1927 as La Scala. The King's in South Methven Street dates back to the summer of 1914 though, following a major fire within five weeks of opening, had to be opened again in 1915. Like the B.B., it too became a bingo hall and still operates as such. One of the best known, though, was the Alhambra in Kinnoull Street which opened in 1922, complete with luncheon and tea rooms, and which, in 1929, had the distinction of showing the first 'talkie' in town, *King of the Khyber Rifles*. The sound quality and the film itself had both been appreciated by the audience which, said the *Perthshire Advertiser*, was felt to augur well 'for the future success of the talkies'. Following a fire of its own in 1956 – almost a rite of passage for cinemas and nightclubs in Perth – the Alhambra reopened as the Gaumont, later still metamorphosing into the Odeon in 1962. Bingo claimed it in the 1980s, after which it became a nightclub before being destroyed by fire in 1993. It was once thought that the advent of television would prove to be the end of cinema and while there is now only one such establishment, the Playhouse, the last to be opened in Perth, the art form continues to reinvent itself and draw in new audiences.

The cinemas of Perth provided good, cheap entertainment for thousands and, in doing so, offered a real alternative to the city's pubs. Dundee cinemas noticeably reduced the levels of drunkenness in that city's streets and there is every reason to believe that the same happened in Perth. Temperance, what Free St Leonard's Church (and, of course, other city churches and organisations) struggled to promote in the nineteenth century, was partially achieved by that church's reincarnation as a cinema in the twentieth. And perhaps there's a sermon there.

BIBLIOGRAPHY

Primary Sources

Minutes of Perth Town Council
Minutes of the Perth Bridge Commissioners
Minutes of the Perthshire Highway Commissioners
Penny, George., Statistical Account of the City of Perth, 1841
Perthshire Courier
Perthshire Advertiser
Perthshire Constitutional
Courier and Advertiser
Perth Paving, Lighting and Cleansing Acts, 1811 and 1819
Perth Harbour Acts, 1830 and 1834
Perth Improvement Act, 1893
Perth Directories, 1837–1939
Perth and Perthshire Registers, 1798–1932
Census returns and statistics for Perth city
Maps of Perth, 1715 to the present

Secondary Sources

Adamson, H., *The Muses Threnodie* (new ed. with notes by James Cant. Perth, James Cant and Robert Morison, 1774)
Auld Perth. (Perth, 1906)
Baxter, P., *The Drama in Perth* (Perth, Thomas Hunter, 1907)
Baxter, P., *Football in Perthshire, past and present*. (Perth, Thomas Hunter, 1898)
Baxter, P., *The Turf of Perth*. (Perth, Thomas Hunter, 1901)
Blair, A., and Doyle, B., *Bristling with Possibilities: the Official History of St Johnstone FC, 1885–1997*. (Perth, Jamieson and Munro, 1997)
Bowler, D.P., *Perth: the Archaeology and Development of a Scottish Burgh*. (Perth, Tayside and Fife Archaeological Committee, 2004)
Bryce, W.M., *The Scottish Grey Friars*. (Edinburgh, William Green, 1909)
Cameron, K.J., *The Schoolmaster Engineer: Adam Anderson of Perth and St Andrews, 1780–1846*. 2nd ed. (Dundee, Abertay Historical Society, 2007)
Cowan, S., *The Ancient Capital of Scotland*. (London, Simpkin, Marshall, Hamilton, Kent and Co., 1904)
Duncan, J., *Perth: a Century of Change*. (Derby, Breedon Books Publishing, 2008)
Duncan, P.J., *The Small Ports and Landing Places of the River Tay, circa 1750 to 1850*. (Unpublished thesis)
Durie, A.J., *The Scottish Linen Industry in the Eighteenth Century*. (Edinburgh, John Donald, 1979)
Easson, D.E., *Medieval Religious Houses: Scotland*. (London, Longmans, 1957)
Farquhar, G.T.S., *The Episcopal History of Perth, 1689–1894*. (Perth, Jackson, 1894)
Fasti Ecclesiae Scoticanae, Presbytery of Perth. Various editions and volumes

Fawcett, R., *A History of Saint John's Kirk of Perth.* (Perth, Friends of St John's Kirk, 1987)

Fechney Industrial School, Perth, *Annual reports*

Fittis, R.S., Numerous volumes of writings, collected articles and newscuttings on the history of Perth

Gifford, J., *The Buildings of Scotland: Perth and Kinross.* (Yale University Press, 2007)

Haldane, A.R.B., *The Great Fishmonger of the Tay: John Richardson of Perth and Pitfour, 1760–1821.* (Dundee, Abertay Historical Society, 1981)

Haynes, N., *Perth and Kinross: an Illustrated Architectural Guide.* (Rutland Press, 2000)

Holdsworth, P. (ed.), *Excavations in the Medieval Burgh of Perth, 1979–1981.* (Edinburgh, Society of Antiquaries of Scotland, 1987)

Hunter, T., *St John's Kirk, Perth: a History.* (Perth, 1932)

Hunter, T., *Woods, Forests and Estates of Perthshire.* (Perth, Henderson, Robertson and Hunter, 1883)

Mackelvie, W., *Annals and Statistics of the United Presbyterian Church.* (Edinburgh, Oliphant, 1873)

Marshall, T.H., *The History of Perth.* (Perth, John Fisher, 1849)

Memorabilia of the City of Perth. (Perth, William Morison, 1806)

Milne, R., *The Blackfriars of Perth.* (Edinburgh, David Douglas, 1893)

Milne, R., *Rental books of King James VI Hospital, Perth.* (Perth, 1891)

Mylne, R.S., *The Master Masons to the Crown of Scotland and Their Works.* (Scott, Ferguson and Burness and Co., 1893)

[New] Statistical Account of Perthshire. (Edinburgh, William Blackwood, 1844)

[Old] Statistical Account of Scotland, 1791–1799. New ed. Vol 11, South and East Perthshire. (Wakefield, EP Publishing, 1976)

Omand, D. (ed.), *The Perthshire Book.* (Edinburgh, Birlinn, 1999)

Peacock, D., *Perth: its Annals and its Archives.* (Perth, Thomas Richardson, 1849)

Penny, G., *Traditions of Perth.* (Perth, Dewar, Sidey, Morison, Peat and Drummond, 1836)

Perth Ladies' House of Refuge for Destitute Girls, *Annual reports*

Perth School Board, *Minutes and annual reports*

Perthshire Advertiser Centenary Number, 12 August 1929

Robertson, I.A., *The Tay Salmon Fisheries Since the Eighteenth Century.* (Glasgow, Cruithne Press, 1998)

Sievright, W., *Historical Sketch of the General Prison for Scotland, at Perth.* (Perth, Alexander Wright, 1894)

Sievwright, W., *Historical Sketch of the Old Depot.* (Perth, Alexander Wright, 1894)

Simpson, W.D., *A Short History of Saint John's Kirk of Perth.* (Perth, Society of Friends of Saint John's Kirk of Perth, 1958)

Small, R., *History of the Congregations of the United Presbyterian Church from 1733 to 1900.* (Edinburgh, David M. Small, 1904)

Smart, E., *History of Perth Academy.* (Perth, 1932)

Society for Relief of Incurables in Perth and Perthshire, *Annual reports*

Stavert, M., *Perth: a Short History.* 2nd ed. (Perth, Perth and Kinross District Libraries, 1991)

Stones, J.A. (ed.), *Three Scottish Carmelite Friaries: Excavations at Aberdeen, Linlithgow and Perth, 1980–1986.* (Edinburgh, Society of Antiquaries of Scotland, 1989)

Taylor, D.B. (ed.), *The Third Statistical Account . . . of Perth and Kinross.* (Scottish Council of Social Service, 1979)

Thomson, A.G., *The Paper Industry in Scotland, 1590–1861.* (Edinburgh, Scottish Academic Press, 1974)

Toner, B., *Mr Mackay's Legacy: St John's School in Perth, 1832–2010.* (Pitlochry, Anna Books, 2010)

Tullibardine, Marchioness of (ed.), *A Military History of Perthshire, 1660–1902.* (Perth, Hay, 1908)

Verschuur, M., *Politics or Religion? The Reformation in Perth, 1540–1570.* (Edinburgh, Dunedin Academic Press, 2006)

INDEX